Market Power, Economic Efficiency, and the Lerner Index

World Scientific–Now Publishers Series in Business

ISSN: 2251-3442

The World Scientific–Now Publishers Series in Business publishes advanced textbooks, research monographs, and edited volumes on a variety of topics in business studies including accounting, entrepreneurship, finance, management, marketing, operations, and strategy. The Series includes both applied and theoretical topics that present current research and represent the state-of-the-art work in their respective fields. Contributed by academic scholars from academic and research institutions worldwide, books published under this Series will be of interest to researchers, doctoral students, and technical professionals.

Published:

The complete list of titles in the series can be found at
https://www.worldscientific.com/series/wsnpsb

(Continued at the end of the book)

World Scientific – Now Publishers Series in Business: **Vol. 19**

Market Power, Economic Efficiency, and the Lerner Index

Editors

Rolf Färe
Oregon State University, USA

Shawna Grosskopf
Oregon State University, USA

Dimitris Margaritis
University of Auckland Business School, New Zealand

Published by

World Scientific Publishing Co. Pte. Ltd.

5 Toh Tuck Link, Singapore 596224

USA office: 27 Warren Street, Suite 401-402, Hackensack, NJ 07601

UK office: 57 Shelton Street, Covent Garden, London WC2H 9HE

and

now publishers Inc.
PO Box 1024
Hanover, MA 02339
USA

Library of Congress Cataloging-in-Publication Data
Names: Färe, Rolf, 1942- editor. | Grosskopf, Shawna, editor. | Margaritis, Dimitris, editor.
Title: Market power, economic efficiency, and the Lerner index /
   [edited by] Rolf Färe, Oregon State University, USA, Shawna Grosskopf,
   Oregon State University, USA, Dimitris Margaritis, University of Auckland
   Business School, New Zealand.
Description: New Jersey : World Scientific, [2024] | Series: World
   Scientific-now publishers series in business, 2251-3442 ; volume 19 |
   Includes bibliographical references and index.
Identifiers: LCCN 2023048984 | ISBN 9789811285929 (hardcover) |
   ISBN 9789811285936 (ebook) | ISBN 9789811285943 (ebook other)
Subjects: LCSH: Production (Economic theory) | Production functions
   (Economic theory) | Industrial productivity.
Classification: LCC HB241 .M354 | DDC 338.001--dc23/eng/20231128
LC record available at https://lccn.loc.gov/2023048984

British Library Cataloguing-in-Publication Data
A catalogue record for this book is available from the British Library.

For any available supplementary material, please visit
https://www.worldscientific.com/worldscibooks/10.1142/13668#t=suppl

Desk Editors: Sanjay Varadharajan/Claire Lum

Typeset by Stallion Press
Email: enquiries@stallionpress.com

Printed in Singapore

Preface

The recent experience with high inflation rates following persistent bouts of massive expansionary fiscal and monetary policies in response to the pandemic crisis amplified by the Russian invasion of Ukraine has increased public scrutiny on market power. In the words of former US Secretary of Labor, Robert Reich, fighting inflation by putting more people out of work via increasing interest rates to cool the economy is cruel, especially in countries like the US where safety nets — including unemployment insurance — are in tatters. To quote Reich from his January 8, 2023 column in *The Guardian*: "The problem *isn't* that wages are rising. The real problem is that corporations have the power to pass those wage increases — along with record profit margins — on to consumers in the form of higher prices. If corporations had to compete vigorously for consumers, they wouldn't be able to do this. Competitors would charge lower prices and grab those consumers away."

Recent increases in interest rates following a tightening of monetary conditions by central banks to combat rising inflationary pressures have also renewed interest in the pass-through of policy rates to retail interest rates. At the center of this debate is the degree of market power in the market for loans recognizing that lending spreads have widened considerably. For example, mortgage spreads are now well above those present during the early stages of the COVID-19 pandemic and are approaching levels last seen during the 2008 financial crisis. Similarly, small business loans are now approaching double-digit levels in many OECD countries for the first time in decades raising concerns about the future state of the global economy.

In this book, we use distance functions as the theoretical and empirical tools to construct Lerner Indexes of market power in both the input and output markets. The use of distance functions enables us to account explicitly for the effects of inefficiency and markups in the evaluation of market power. Part A of this book (Chapters 1–3) focuses on the theory, whereas Part B (Chapters 4–7) provides a menu of applications using parametric forms of the distance functions to construct measures of firm efficiency and market power.

Chapter 1 begins with an overview of the axioms that we need to develop rigorous descriptions of technology and their associated representations in the form of distance functions. The chapter also introduces the Nerlovian measure of profit efficiency, which we use to derive the indexes of monopoly and monopsony power.

Chapter 2 introduces the Lerner Index of market power beginning with the single-output Lerner Index in conjunction with production theoretic efficiency indexes, including several decompositions. We then turn to the case of multiple outputs, which introduces aggregation issues, both across goods and across firms to form an industry index.

In Chapter 3, we turn to construct the measure of market power in input markets, beginning with the single input case. We derive an economic efficiency interpretation with associated decompositions. We generalize our input index to the multiple input case which introduces the issue of aggregation both across inputs and firms.

In Chapter 4, Färe, Grosskopf, Hasannasab and Margaritis introduce an integrative framework to study bank revenue efficiency and market structure in the Central and Eastern European (CEE) deposits market. Specifically, they use output distance functions to develop a Lerner-type index capturing deviations from competitive behavior in input markets. They show how this index may be estimated using information on input and output quantities and output prices. They find that riskier banks, such as those with more impaired loans, and banks that rely more on deposits to fund their assets exert less monopsony power for deposits. Bank profitability and revenue efficiency on the other hand are positively associated with monopsony power.

In Chapter 5, Färe, Hasannasab, Karagiannis and Margaritis take a different look at bank efficiency and market structure for CEE banks. Specifically, they use input distance functions to develop an output-oriented Lerner-type index capturing deviations from competitive behavior in the market for bank loans. They show how this index may be estimated using information on input and output quantities, operating cost and interest income on loans. They find that greater bank competition is not only associated with lower bank risk but also with higher profits and operating efficiency.

In Chapter 6, Weber and Wu investigate the price efficiency of Chinese banks using a multi-product Lerner Index. Banks in China are dominated by state-owned commercial banks and until recently have been subject to price controls which set minimum interest rates that banks can charge on loans and maximum interest rates that they can pay for deposits. To construct the Lerner Index, they calculate marginal costs from an estimated cost function and the shadow output prices from an estimated translog input distance function. They find that state-owned commercial banks have significant market power in loans but overproduce securities investments and they hypothesize that the overproduction of securities investments might be due to risk-based capital requirements. They also find that other private banks produce a portfolio of loans that is consistent with marginal cost pricing.

In Chapter 7, Bishop, Färe, Grosskopf, Hayes, Weber and Wetzel move away from the analysis of market power in the financial sector and focus instead on a public sector application, namely whether German theatres exploit monopoly power. Using the same general model employed in Chapter 6, they provide estimates of generally unknown price of the public service by estimating shadow output prices from a translog input distance function. These are compared to marginal costs estimated from the cost function in order to construct the Lerner Index. They assume that theatres produce performances and spectators and find that they have monopoly power over spectators but overproduce performances. Increasing spectators per performance would improve efficiency. They also find that the large public subsidies provided to these theatres are negatively related to market power.

About the Editors

Shawna Grosskopf is Professor Emerita at Oregon State University and Adjunct Professor at Centre for Environmental Resource Economics in Umea, Sweden. Her research includes work in performance measurement with applications in education, environmental productivity, public sector performance and health. She serves as an Associate Editor for *Journal of Productivity Analysis* and is listed in Research.com Best Economics and Finance Scientists; ranked 141 in the world, 107 in the U.S.

Rolf G. Färe received his engineering degree from Gymnasiet in Helsingborg, Sweden. Like some other Europeans of his generation — W.M. 'Terence' Gorman comes to mind — he never earned a standard PhD degree but earned a Filosofie Licentiat degree and eventually a Docent in Economics from Lund University under Professor Björn Thalberg. He left Lund to study at U.C. Berkeley for two years under Professor Ronald W. Shephard. It wasn't, however, as difficult as the year he spent doing mandatory military service at the Defence Research Institute in Stockholm. He returned to the U.S. and has had the good luck of working and writing with many scholars in production economics as well as advising quite a few PhD students, many of whom also became his co-authors.

 **Dimitris Margaritis** is Professor of Finance at the University of Auckland Business School. He served as Advisor and Head of Research at the Reserve Bank of New Zealand and was subsequently appointed as the Bank's Senior Research Fellow. He was a member of the World Bank's project on Financial Reform and the leader of the New Zealand Enterprise Efficiency and Productivity project funded by the Foundation for Research, Science and Technology. He has published extensively in the international refereed literature in banking, corporate finance, asset pricing, performance measurement and productivity analysis. He served as Guest Editor of the *Journal of Productivity Analysis* and is currently on the Editorial Board of *Accounting and Finance*.

About the Contributors

Maryam Hasannasab is a Lecturer in Finance at the University of Auckland Business School. She holds a PhD in Applied Mathematics (Operations Research) from Kharazmi University of Tehran and is currently completing a PhD in Finance at the University of Auckland. She has published extensively in the efficiency and productivity area including several papers in the *European Journal of Operational Research*, *Annals of Operations Research* and *Journal of Productivity Analysis*. In 2019, she received the University of Auckland, Business School Research Excellence Award for Outstanding Performance by an Emerging Researcher.

Giannis Karagiannis is Professor in the Department of Economics at the University of Macedonia, Thessaloniki, Greece, where he is teaching microeconomics. He received his BA in Economics from the University of Macedonia, Greece, and his MSc and PhD in Agricultural Economics from the University of Saskatchewan, Canada. He was co-editor of the *European Review of Agricultural Economics* (2013–2018) and he is Associate Editor of the *Journal of Productivity Analysis*. He is working in the field of production economics and in particular, on performance evaluation, efficiency measurement and productivity analysis and he has published several theoretical and empirical papers in this area.

Bill Weber is Professor Emeritus of Economics at Southeast Missouri State University where he taught for 36 years. His research interests are in shadow pricing of non-market goods and in measuring producer performance with applications in environmental economics, primary/secondary education, higher education and banking. He has published papers in *Journal of Econometrics*, *Review of Economics and Statistics*, *Management Science*, *Omega* and *Journal of Banking and Finance*.

Chen Wu is an Associate Professor of Economics at Southeast Missouri State University where she teaches undergraduate economic courses and supervises MBA applied research projects. Her research interests are in applied econometrics, international trade, development economics and banking. She has published articles in various journals, including *International Journal of Forecasting*, *Studies in Nonlinear Dynamics & Econometrics* and *Economics Letters*.

Kristina Bishop holds a PhD in Economics from Southern Methodist University and a master's in statistics and a bachelor's in mathematics education from Brigham Young University. She was a Niemi Fellow with the George W. Bush Institute and a research fellow at the BYU Law School. Her research interests are in the fields of labor and family economics, innovation and applied econometrics.

Kathy Hayes earned her PhD degree in 1980 from Syracuse University. She started at SMU in the fall of 1985 in the economics department of Dedman College. Besides being a Professor of Economics, she has worked as Associate Dean, Interim Department Chair and Director of Undergraduate Studies. She teaches two public economics classes: Federal Expenditures and State and Local Public Finance. Her primary research focus is on Economics of Education.

Heike Wetzel is Professor of Microeconomics and Empirical Energy Economics at the University of Kassel. She studied business administration at the Leuphana University of Lüneburg. From 2003 to 2009, she worked as a research assistant at the Chair of Economic Policy at the Leuphana University of Lüneburg. In 2008, she received her doctorate in economics at the Leuphana University of Lüneburg on the efficiency and productivity of European railways. From 2009 to 2014, she worked as a post-doctoral researcher at the Chair of Energy Economics and as an affiliated researcher at the Institute of Energy Economics at the University of Cologne. From 2014 to 2016, she was scientific director of the department 'Decentralized Energy Markets' at the IdE Institute for Decentralized Energy Technologies in Kassel. Her research interests include applied energy and regulatory economics as well as empirical efficiency and productivity analysis.

https://doi.org/10.1142/9789811285936_fmatter

Contents

Part A

Lerner Indexes: Theoretical Underpinnings

Chapter 1

Basic Production Theory[*]

Rolf G. Färe[†], Shawna Grosskopf[†], and Dimitris Margaritis[‡]

[†]Oregon State University, Corvallis, USA
[‡]University of Auckland, Auckland, New Zealand

1. Introduction

In this chapter, we introduce the economic concepts that we employ throughout this book, which includes a fairly detailed overview of "modern" production theory. We begin with an overview of the axioms that we need to develop rigorous descriptions of technology and their associated representations as functions. The functions we introduce first are distance functions, which are the multiple output cousins of production functions. Since our goal is to provide theoretically and empirically consistent measures of market power, we include parametric functional forms that can be used to estimate these functions in Section 4.

We ultimately introduce the Nerlovian measure of profit efficiency, which we use to derive the indexes of monopoly and monopsony power.

2. The Axiomatic Technology

We begin with our notation: inputs are defined as a vector of non-negative real numbers $x = (x_1, \ldots, x_N) \in \Re_+^N$. We note that taking inputs as real numbers implies divisibility, which may be unintuitive; e.g., π is a possible value, which is awkward if the input is labor. However, see Bobzin (1998) for how one may model technology with indivisible inputs and outputs.

---

[*]We thank Vic Tremblay for his helpful comments.

3

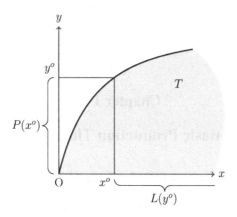

Figure 1. The Technology Sets

Similarly, we denote outputs as a vector of non-negative real numbers $y = (y_1, \ldots, y_M) \in \mathfrak{R}_+^M$.

We introduce three equivalent set representations of the technology, namely

$$T = \{(x, y) : x \text{ can produce } y\}, \text{ the technology set,}$$

$$P(x) = \{y : (x, y) \in T\}, x \in \mathfrak{R}_+^N, \text{ the output set,}$$

$$L(y) = \{x : (x, y) \in T\}, y \in \mathfrak{R}_+^M, \text{ the input set.}$$

We illustrate these sets for the single input and output case in Figure 1, where $P(x^o)$ is part of the vertical axis and $L(y^o)$ is part of the horizontal axis. Specifically, for this figure

$$P(x^o) = \{y : y \leqq y^o, y^o \in T\} \quad \text{and} \quad L(y^o) = \{x : x \geqq x^o, x^0 \in T\}$$

Using our definitions of our sets, we can now verify that they are equivalent representations of technology. Let $(x, y) \in T$, then by the definitions of $y \in P(x)$ and $x \in L(y)$, we have

$$(x, y) \in T \Rightarrow y \in P(x) \quad \text{and} \quad x \in L(y)$$

Next, let $y \in P(x)$, then by the definition of T, $(x, y) \in T$. Similarly, if $x \in L(y)$, then $(x, y) \in T$. We can now state the following:

Proposition 2.1 $(x, y) \in T \Leftrightarrow x \in L(y) \Leftrightarrow y \in P(x)$.

Although this is not intended as a book on axiomatic production theory, it is useful to list and state the most common axioms so we can readily refer to them as needed. Since we have established the equivalence of our three reference sets, for each axiom we will choose the set which provides the clearest illustration.

The first two conditions we introduce are related to the notion of *inactivity*:

A.1 $(0, 0) \in T$.
A.2 $0 \in P(x)$, for all $x \in \mathfrak{R}_+^N$.

The first condition states that zero input and zero output is a feasible activity. The second tells us that producing zero output is feasible for all input vectors. Clearly, since $0 \in \mathfrak{R}_+^N$, A.2 $\Rightarrow$ A.1.

Convexity is required to prove duality theorems, as well as to work with subdifferentials, see Rockafellar (1970). As we will see, convexity may be imposed on any of our technology sets, T, $P(x)$, or $L(y)$, and these conditions differ. Beginning with convexity of T:

A.3 If $(x, y), (x', y') \in T, 0 \leq \lambda \leq 1$ implies that $(1 - \lambda)(x, y) + \lambda(x', y') \in T$, then T is convex.

Note that since $(0, 0) \in T$ from A.1, then for any $(x, y) \in T$ and $0 \leq \lambda \leq 1, (\lambda x, \lambda y) \in T$ and hence the technology exhibits non-increasing returns to scale (NIRS).

If we choose $x = x'$ in A.3, then

A.4 $(1 - \lambda)(y) + \lambda(y') \in P(x)$ and then the output set is convex.

If we choose $y = y'$, then the input set is convex, i.e.,

A.5 $(1 - \lambda)(x) + \lambda(x') \in L(y)$.

Thus, it is clear that T convex implies that $P(x)$ and $L(y)$ are convex. However, the converse is not necessarily true, which is illustrated in Figure 2.

Under optimization, for an optimizer to exist it must belong to the set over which optimization occurs, and that set must be closed. For example, if the objective is to maximize profit, then T must be closed, leading to the following axioms:

A.6 T is closed, i.e., $(x^n, y^n) \in T$ for all $n = 1, \ldots, \infty$, and $(x^n, y^n) \rightarrow (x^o, y^o)$, then $(x^0, y^0) \in T$.

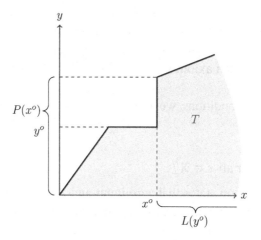

Figure 2. *P(x)* **and** *L(y)* **are Convex but not** *T*

With respect to the other two technology sets $P(x)$ and $L(y)$ we assume that

A.7 $P(x)$ is closed, i.e., $y^n \rightarrow y^o$, with $y^n \in P(x)$ then $y^o \in P(x)$

and

A.8 $L(y)$ is closed, i.e., $x^n \rightarrow x^o$, with $x^n \in L(y)$ then $x^o \in L(y)$

Clearly by taking $x^n = x^o$ then it follows that A.6 implies A.7. Similarly by taking $y^n = y^o$ then A.6 implies A.8. The converse need not hold.

Turning to *monotonicity/disposability*, i.e., referring to "throwing away" or freely disposing of output or overusing or leaving inputs idle, we begin with the technology set T:

A.9 $(x, y) \in T, x' \geqq x, y' \leqq y \Rightarrow (x', y') \in T$

In words, it is feasible to produce fewer than the maximum feasible output given inputs, and it is also feasible to use too much or waste inputs for given outputs. These disposability assumptions are important for duality to hold, and what types of shadow prices are feasible.

Turning to disposability with respect to our output and input sets, we have

A.10 $y \in P(x), y' \leqq y \Rightarrow y' \in P(x)$

and

A.11 $\quad x \in L(y), x' \geqq x \Rightarrow x' \in L(y)$

By taking $x' = x$ A.9 implies A.10, and similarly taking $y' = y$, A.9 implies A.11.

Suppose that some outputs are considered to be undesirable such as polluting emissions, then the assumption that these outputs are strongly or costlessly disposable may be controversial, or in conflict with regulatory limits. A weaker assumption may be employed in these cases:

A.10W $\quad y \in P(x), 0 \leqq \lambda \leqq 1 \Rightarrow \lambda y \in P(x)$.

We refer to this axiom as weak disposability of outputs. Note that if $0 \in P(x)$, A.2 and $P(x)$ is convex A.4, then the outputs are weakly disposable. It has been shown, see Färe and Primont (1995), that weak disposability of outputs is necessary and sufficient for the output distance function — to be introduced presently — to completely represent the technology $P(x)$.

On the input side we defined weak disposability as

A.11W $\quad x \in L(y), \lambda \geqq 1 \Rightarrow \lambda x \in L(y)$.

Mirroring weak output disposability, this is a necessary and sufficient condition for the input distance function to represent the technology $L(y)$. Note that strong disposability of inputs precludes the possibility of congestion, whereas weak disposability does not. We illustrate with a suitably restricted Cobb–Douglas production function

$$y = \begin{cases} x_1^{\alpha}(x_2 - ax_1)^{1-\alpha} & \text{if } (x_2 - ax_1) \geqq 0, \\ 0 & \text{otherwise.} \end{cases}$$

This function is illustrated in Figure 3.

The idea that finite inputs can only produce finite output is stated as, i.e., for each y and $y' \in P(x)$,

A.12

$$\sup\{(y - y')\} < \infty$$

i.e., $P(x)$ is bounded.

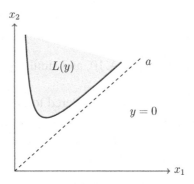

Figure 3. A Weakly Disposable Production Function; x_1 is the Congesting Input

We would also require that technology satisfy what has been called the assumption of "no free lunch", i.e.,

A.13 $(x, y) \in T$ and $x = 0 \Rightarrow y = 0$

which states that without positive input, one cannot produce positive outputs. Put differently one can state

$$(x, y) \in T, \quad y \geq 0 \Rightarrow x \geq 0$$

i.e., to produce outputs requires inputs.

The next three axioms refer to what is known as scale properties. We distinguish among three concepts: Non-increasing (NIRS), Constant (CRS), and Non-decreasing (NDRS) Returns to Scale:

A.14 $(x, y) \in T$ and $0 \leq \lambda \leq 1 \Rightarrow (\lambda x, \lambda y) \in T$ (NIRS),

A.15 $(x, y) \in T$ and $\lambda \geq 0 \Rightarrow (\lambda x, \lambda y) \in T$ (CRS),

A.16 $(x, y) \in T$ and $\lambda \geq 1 \Rightarrow (\lambda x, \lambda y) \in T$ (NDRS).

Since $(x, y) \in T \Leftrightarrow x \in L(y) \Leftrightarrow y \in P(x)$, A.14–A.16 may also be formulated with respect to $L(y)$ and $P(x)$.

3. Distance Functions

Distance functions appear as far back as Maurice Frechèt's (1906) PhD thesis. The name — distance function — was coined by Felix Hausdorff, according to Google Scholar.

We employ two basic types of distance functions commonly used in economics, namely radial and directional distance functions. Radial distance functions were introduced into economics by Shephard (1953, 1970), importantly in association with duality theory. The directional distance functions are associated with Luenberger (1995) and Chambers *et al.* (1998). They have their origin in the Allais (1943) surplus function.

Although the directional distance function is the most general in the sense that the radial distance functions are special cases, we begin our discussion with the more familiar Shephard distance functions. These provide functional representations of the input and output sets. The input distance function is defined on the input set, i.e.,

$$D_i(y, x) = \sup\{\lambda : x/\lambda \in L(y)\}$$

By its definition it is homogeneous of degree +1 input quantities,

$$D_i(y, \theta x) = \theta D_i(y, x), \theta > 0$$

If inputs are weakly disposable, the function is a complete representation of the input set, see Färe and Primont (1995),

$$L(y) = \{x : D_i(y, x) \geqq 1\}$$

The representation property implies that the axioms A.1–A.16 can be expressed in terms of $D_i(y, x)$, which we leave to the reader.

Given an output set $P(x)$, the output distance function is defined as

$$D_o(x, y) = \inf\{\theta : y/\theta \in P(x)\}$$

By definition this function is homogeneous of degree +1 in output quantities, i.e.,

$$D_o(x, \lambda y) = \lambda D_o(x, y), \lambda > 0$$

If outputs are weakly disposable, the output distance function is a complete representation of the output set,

$$P(x) = \{y : D_o(x, y) \leqq 1\}$$

hence all the axioms A.1–A.16 can be expressed in terms of $D_o(x, y)$.

Note that there is no radial distance function defined on the technology set T. It is straightforward to see why radial expansions and contractions are problematic relative to T: A ray from the origin in the input–output space may not "hit" technology T. However, as we will see, what has come to be known as directional distance functions can readily be defined on T.[1] The directional distance function is defined as

$$\vec{D}_T(x, y; g_x, g_y) = \sup\{\beta : (x - \beta g_x, y + \beta g_y) \in T\}$$

From its definition it satisfies the *Translation Property*, i.e.,

$$\vec{D}_T(x - \alpha g_x, y + \alpha g_y; g_x, g_y) = \vec{D}_T(x, y; g_x, g_y) - \alpha, \alpha \in \Re$$

In contrast to the radial distance functions, the scaling factor is on the directional vectors g_x, g_y, rather than on the observed input or output quantities. These vectors determine the direction in which the frontier of T is approached. Typically these are chosen by the researcher, but they may also be endogenized, as, for example, in Färe *et al.* (2014).

If inputs and outputs are strongly disposable, then the directional distance function satisfies *The Representation Property*, i.e.,

$$\vec{D}_T(x, y; g_x, g_y) \geqq 0 \quad \text{if and only if } (x, y) \in T$$

This property allows us to formulate the axioms A.1–A.16 in terms of the directional technology distance function, $\vec{D}_T(x, y; g_x, g_y)$.

Two other directional distance functions may be derived as special cases of $\vec{D}_T(x, y; g_x, g_y)$. By setting one of the directional vectors equal to zero, we can specify directional output and directional input distance functions. If we choose $g_x = 0$, the directional output distance function is defined as

$$\vec{D}_o(x, y; g_y) = \sup\{\beta : (y + \beta g_y) \in P(x)\}$$

noting that $y \in P(x)$ if and only if $(x, y) \in T$.

Similarly, if we choose $g_y = 0$, the directional input distance function may be defined as

$$\vec{D}_i(y, x; g_x) = \sup\{\beta : (x - \beta g_x) \in L(y)\}$$

---

[1]Other non-radial functions can be used to project to the boundary of T. One example is the hyperbolic or graph functions, see Färe *et al.* (1985).

Thus we have the following relationships:

$$\vec{D}_o(x, y; g_y) = \vec{D}_T(x, y; 0, g_y)$$

and

$$\vec{D}_i(y, x; g_x) = \vec{D}_T(x, y; g_x, 0)$$

These equalities imply that the directional input and output distance functions satisfy the translation property in g_x and g_y, respectively. In addition, they have the following representation properties:

$$\vec{D}_o(x, y; g_y) \geqq 0 \quad \text{if and only if } y \in P(x)$$

and

$$\vec{D}_i(y, x; g_x) \geqq 0 \quad \text{if and only if } x \in L(y)$$

Next we ask how the directional distance functions are related to the radial Shephard distance functions. By setting the directional vectors equal to the respective input and output quantities, one can show that

$$\vec{D}_o(x, y; y) = \frac{1}{D_o(x, y)} - 1$$

and

$$\vec{D}_i(x, y; x) = 1 - \frac{1}{D_i(y, x)}$$

4. Parameterizing the Distance Functions

When the distance functions are used in econometric applications, these distance functions are typically estimated using specific functional forms. Here we assume that those functional forms should be of the flexible type. These have several different names: Chambers (1988) calls them generalized quadratic functions, whereas Diewert (2002) refers to them as as transformed quadratic and Färe and Sung (1986) dub them second-order Taylor series approximations. More specifically, consider the two variable case (q_1, q_2) (of course this can be generalized to any finite number), where the function takes the form

$$F : \mathfrak{R}^2 \to F(q_1, q_2) \in \mathfrak{R} \quad \text{with } h : \mathfrak{R} \to \mathfrak{R} \text{ and } \rho : \mathfrak{R} \to \mathfrak{R}$$

then

$$F(q_1, q_2) = \rho^{-1} \left(a_o + \sum_{i=1}^{2} a_i h(q_i) + \sum_{i=1}^{2} \sum_{j=1}^{2} a_{ij} h(q_i) h(q_j) \right)$$

where the $a's$ are real constants. If $a_o = a_{ij} = 0$, then the function reduces to what Aczél (1966) refers to as a quasi-linear function.

Recall that the radial type distance functions are homogeneous of degree one in the scaled vector. In terms of our function F, this translates into

$$F(\lambda q) = \lambda F(q), \quad q \in \mathfrak{R}^2, \ \lambda > 0$$

In contrast, the directional distance functions satisfy the translation property which in terms of F reads as

$$F(q + \alpha q) = F(q) + \alpha, \quad q \in \mathfrak{R}^2, \ \alpha \in \mathfrak{R}$$

If we impose these conditions on the generalized quadratic function, we have two functional equations that have been solved. For the homogeneous case, Färe and Sung (1986) found two solutions, namely the translog

$$F(q_1, q_2) = a_o + \sum_{i=1}^{2} a_i \ln(q_i) + \sum_{i=1}^{2} \sum_{j=1}^{2} a_{ij} \ln(q_i) \ln(q_j)$$

and the mean of order ρ:

$$F(q_1, q_2) = \left(a_{11} q_1^{\rho/2} + a_{22} q_2^{\rho/2} + a_{12} q_1^{\rho/2} q_2^{\rho/2} \right)^{1/\rho}$$

Note that the second solution — mean of order ρ — has only second-order terms, whereas the translog has both first and second order terms. A disadvantage with the translog is that no variable can take a zero value, since $\ln(0)$ is not a real number.

The functional equation obtained when we impose the translation property on the generalized quadratic function also yields two solutions, see Färe and Lundgren (2006), including the quadratic function

$$F(q_1, q_2) = \alpha_o + \sum_{i=1}^{2} a_i(q_i) + \sum_{i=1}^{2}\sum_{j=1}^{2} a_{ij}(q_i)(q_j)$$

and an unnamed function

$$F(q_1, q_2) = 1/2\alpha \ln \sum_{i=1}^{2}\sum_{j=1}^{2} a_{ij} \exp(\lambda q_i) \exp(\lambda q_j)$$

Again, the quadratic function has both first- and second-order parameters, but the other has only second-order parameters. Note that the quadratic form allows some variables to be zero.

5. The Nerlovian Profit Efficiency Measure

Based on earlier work by Nerlove (1965), Chambers *et al.* (1998) developed what they called a Nerlovian profit efficiency measure. In this chapter, we rely on this measure to derive the Lerner monopoly and monopsony measures of market power.

Define the profit function as

$$\Pi(p, w) = \sup\{py - wx : (x, y) \in T\}$$

where p is a vector of output prices and w a vector of input prices.

One can show that it is related to the directional technology distance function as

$$\Pi(p, w) \geqq py - wx + \vec{D}_T(x, y; g_x, g_y)(pg_y + wg_x)$$

where g_y and g_x are directional vectors. Rearranging this expression yields

$$\vec{D}_T(x, y; g_x, g_y) \leqq \frac{\Pi(p, w) - (py - wx)}{pg_y + wg_x}$$

Chambers *et al.* (2014) define the right-hand side of the above expression as the Nerlovian profit efficiency measure:

$$\aleph = \frac{\Pi(p, w) - (py - wx)}{pg_y + wg_x}$$

We interpret this measure as the difference between maximal profit and observed profit $(py - wx)$, normalized by the value of the direction vectors.

https://doi.org/10.1142/9789811285936_0002

Chapter 2

Monopoly Power, Output Lerner Indexes[*]

Rolf G. Färe[†], Shawna Grosskopf[†], and Dimitris Margaritis[‡]

†Oregon State University, Corvallis, USA
‡University of Auckland, Auckland, New Zealand

1. Introduction

In this chapter, we introduce our indexes of monopoly power. We begin with the classic, single-output Lerner Index and connect it to production theoretic efficiency indexes, including several decompositions. We then turn to the case of multiple outputs, which introduces aggregation issues, both across goods and across firms to form an industry index. We conclude this chapter with a discussion of estimation issues.

2. The Single-Output Case

Following the notation used by Lerner (1934, p. 169), let P be the output price of the single good and C be its marginal cost. Then the Lerner measure of monopoly power is defined as

$$\pounds_o = \frac{P - C}{P}, \tag{1}$$

i.e., the (percent or normalized) difference between output price P and marginal cost (C) of the single output. We think of $\pounds_o$ as an output-oriented Lerner Index in the same sense as we think of output oriented distance functions.

---

[*]We thank Vic Tremblay for his helpful comments.

In order to generalize and rationalize this index, we turn our attention to the underlying technology, where we begin with the input set $L(y)$ defined as

$$L(y) = \{x : x \text{ can produce } y\}$$

In order to define the cost function, let input prices be $w \in \mathfrak{R}_+^N$, then the cost function is defined as

$$C(y, w) = \min_x \{wx : x \in L(y)\}$$

and

$$C = \frac{\partial C}{\partial y}(y, w) = \text{MC}$$

is the marginal cost function.

Returning to the single-output index

$$\pounds_o = \frac{P - C}{P}$$

Lerner (1923, p. 169) notes that "…this formula looks like the inverse of the formula for the elasticity of demand." Which follows from "…marginal cost replaces the item marginal receipt." Note that what he refers to as marginal receipt is what we commonly refer to as marginal revenue. Taking $P = p$, we define the (total) revenue function as

$$R(x, p) = \max\{py : x \in L(y)\}$$

and the associated marginal revenue is

$$\text{MR} = \frac{\partial R(x, p)}{\partial x}$$

Following Perloff et al. (2007, p. 6), or Färe et al. (2012, p. 141), this function has the following property:

$$\text{MR} = p \left(1 + \frac{1}{\epsilon_d}\right)$$

where ϵ_d is the elasticity of demand.

In equilibrium,

$$MR = MC$$

where we again treat $P = p$ and conclude that the Lerner Index $£_o$ equals

$$£_o = -\frac{1}{\epsilon_d}$$

see also Lerner (1934, p. 169).

Under free competition,

$$MR = p = MC$$

which follows from

$$\max_y \; py - C(y, w)$$

$$\frac{\partial}{\partial y} = p - \frac{\partial C(y, w)}{\partial y} = 0$$

Thus in competition, when the price is taken as given by the firm, we have

$$£_o = \frac{p - \frac{\partial C(y,w)}{\partial y}}{p} = 0$$

Why is the index normalized by p? Perloff *et al.* (2007, pp. 1–2) argue that the normalization by p is to make the index independent of unit of measurement.[1]

Next we turn to the connection of the Lerner Index to production theoretic efficiency indexes. Chambers *et al.* (2014) proved that the Lerner Index can be derived from the Nerlovian profit indicator, which allows us to provide the Lerner Index with an efficiency interpretation.

---

[1] Note that from the theory of dual spaces $\frac{\partial C(y,w)}{\partial y}$ belongs to price space, i.e., in the same space as p, assuring independence of unit of measurement, see Färe *et al.* (2019).

Let $\Pi(p, w)$ be a profit function defined as

$$\Pi(p, w) = \max\{py - wx : x \in L(y)\}$$
$$= \max\{py - wx : (x, y) \in T\}$$

where T is the technology set

$$T = \{(x, y) : x \in L(y)\}$$

which can be represented by the directional distance function

$$\vec{D}_T(x, y; g_x, g_y) = \max\{\beta : (y + \beta g_y, x - \beta g_x) \in T\}$$

Denote observed profit by Π^o and the directional output and input vectors by g_y and g_x, then the Nerlovian indicator takes the form

$$\aleph = \frac{\Pi(p, w) - \Pi^o}{pg_y + wg_x}$$

i.e., the difference between maximal profit $\Pi(p, w)$ and observed profit Π^o, normalized by the "value" of output and input prices p and w.

To demonstrate the connection between the Nerlovian indicator and the Lerner Index, let $C(y, w)$ be a cost function and py the observed revenue. We may then write the Nerlovian indicator as the following maximization problem:

$$\aleph = \max_y \frac{py - C(y, w) - \Pi^o}{p}$$

where we have taken the directional vector to be $g_x = 1, g_y = 0$. The associated first-order condition to this problem is

$$\frac{p - \frac{\partial C(w, y)}{\partial y}}{p} = \pounds_o$$

i.e., the Lerner Index.

Earlier we showed that the Lerner Index can be given an elasticity interpretation:

$$\pounds_o = -\frac{1}{\epsilon_d}$$

Chambers *et al.* (2014) provide an economic efficiency interpretation, an alternative which does not require that MR $=$ MC. To see this, let

$$P(x) = \{y : x \text{ can produce } y\} = \{y : (x, y) \in T\}$$

be the output set. Shephard's output distance function is defined relative to this set as

$$D_o(x, y) = \inf\{\theta : y/\theta \in P(x)\}$$

This function is homogeneous of degree $+1$ in outputs, and under weak disposability of output,[2] the distance function is a complete representation of the technology:

$$P(x) = \{y : D_o(x, y) \leqq 1\}$$

The revenue function

$$R(x, p) = \max\{py : y \in P(x)\}$$

may now be defined in terms of the output distance function

$$R(x, p) = \max\{py : D_o(x, y) \leqq 1\}$$

From duality theory, it follows that

$$py = D_o(x, y)R(x, p)$$

and since $D_o(x, y)$ is homogeneous of degree $+1$ in output, we have

$$py = yD_o(x, 1)R(x, p)$$

or

$$p = D_o(x, 1)R(x, p)$$

---

[2] Given $y \in P(x), \theta \in [0, 1] \Rightarrow \theta y \in P(x)$.

We may now derive our decomposition of the Lerner Index as

$$
£_o = \frac{p - \frac{\partial C(y,w)}{\partial y}}{p}
$$

$$
= 1 - \frac{\partial C(y,w)}{\partial y} \frac{1}{D_o(x,1)R(x,p)}
$$

$$
= 1 - \frac{\partial C(y,w)}{\partial y} \frac{yC(y,w)}{yC(y,w)D_o(x,1)R(x,p)}
$$

$$
= 1 - \epsilon_C \frac{1}{D_o(x,y)} \frac{1}{R(x,p)/C(y,w)} \tag{2}
$$

where $\epsilon_C = \frac{\partial C(y,w)}{\partial y}\frac{y}{C(y,p)}$ is the cost elasticity, $\frac{1}{D_o(x,y)}$ is the Farrell output measure of technical efficiency (Farrell, 1957) and $\frac{R(x,p)}{C(y,w)}$ is the Georgescu-Roegen (1951) measure of the "return to the dollar".

Thus without assuming that we have MR $=$ MC, we have a decomposition of the Lerner Index based in efficiency analysis. Building on Bogetoft *et al.* (2006), Mantori (2015) shows that given that the technology is input homothetic, the Lerner Index may be given an additional decomposition. Kutlu and Sickles (2012) provide a dynamic stochastic frontier approach to estimating the role of efficiency in identifying market power.

In the special case of CRS, our expression (2.2) takes an interesting form. Recalling that under CRS the cost function may be written as

$$
C(y,w) = yC(1,w)
$$

Thus it follows that

$$
\epsilon_c = 1
$$

Moreover, under CRS, maximum profit is zero, hence

$$
C(y,w) = R(x,p)
$$

where $R(x,p)$ is the revenue function, which implies that the Georgescu-Roegen measure equals 1. From this, we conclude that

$$
£_o = 1 - \frac{1}{D_o(x,y)}
$$

and in this case with technical efficiency, i.e., $D_o(x, y) = 1$, it follows that $£_o = 0$.

3. Multi-Output Lerner Indexes and Their Aggregation

Turning to the multi-output case, we begin by substituting partial derivatives for the derivative from the single-output case. Following Baumol *et al.* (1982), Panzer and Willig (1982) or Perloff *et al.* (2007), the $m = 1, \ldots, M$ product Lerner Index is defined as

$$£_{om} = \frac{p_m - \frac{\partial C(y, w)}{\partial y_m}}{p_m}, \quad m = 1, \ldots, M$$

where $(p_1, \ldots, p_M) \in \Re_+^M$ are the prices of the outputs $y \in \Re_+^M$. The marginal cost function is defined on

$$C(y, w) = \min_x \{wx : x \in L(y)\}$$

where again y is a vector of outputs $y \in \Re_+^M$.

As in the single-output case, $£_{om}, m = 1, \ldots, M$, can be given an elasticity of demand interpretation (Perloff *et al.* 2007, p. 6),

$$£_{om} = -\frac{1}{\epsilon_{d_m}}, \quad m = 1, \ldots, M$$

where ϵ_{d_m} is the demand elasticity for good m. Paralleling the single output case,

$$\mathrm{MR}_m = \mathrm{MC}_m, \quad m = 1, \ldots, M$$

i.e., in equilibrium the marginal revenue for each m is equal to its marginal cost.

Let

$$\aleph = \frac{\Pi(p, w) - \Pi^o}{pg_y + wg_x}$$

be the Nerlovian multi-product indicator. Note that

$$pg_y = \sum_{m=1}^{M} p_m g_{y_m}$$

ℵ may be derived as a maximization problem

$$\aleph = \max_{y_1,\dots,y_M} \frac{\sum_{m=1}^{M} p_m y_m - C(y,w) - \Pi^o}{\sum_{m=1}^{M} p_m g_m + w g_x}$$

Choosing $g_m = 0$ for all m except for $g_m = 1$, and setting $g_x = 0$, the resulting first-order condition with respect to m is

$$\frac{p_m - \frac{\partial C(y,w)}{\partial y_m}}{p_m}$$

which equals $£_{om}$. Thus each good's Lerner Index may be derived from the Nerlovian indicator.

One may aggregate the output specific indexes $£_{om}$ into a total index with shares as weights, i.e.,

$$s_m = \frac{p_m y_m}{\sum_{m=1}^{M} p_m y_m} \geqq 0, \quad \sum_{m=1}^{M} s_m = 1$$

and

$$£_o^M = \sum_{m=1}^{M} s_m \left(\frac{p_m - \frac{\partial C(y,w)}{\partial y_m}}{p_m} \right)$$

$$= \sum_{m=1}^{M} s_m £_{om} \qquad (3)$$

see Färe and Karagiannis (2021).

As in the single output case, we can give the multi-output index a component-wise efficiency interpretation. This requires some new definitions and notation. We use y_{-m} to denote the output vector $(y_1, \dots, y_{m-1}, y_{m+1}, \dots, y_M)$. Then let

$$\mathrm{SD}_o^m(x, y_m, y_{-m}) = \min\{\theta : (y_1, \dots, y_m/\theta, \dots, y_M) \in P(x)\}$$

be the mth component Shephard output distance function. Let p_m be the price of output m, then the revenue function for the mth output is

$$R^m(x, p_m, p_{-m}) = \max\{p_m y_m \ (y_1, \dots, y_m, \dots, y_M) \in P(x)\}$$

One may prove that

$$p_m y_m = \text{SD}_o^m(x, y_m, y_{-m}) R^m(x, p_m, p_{-m})$$

Since SD_o^m is homogeneous of degree +1 in y_m, it follows that

$$p_m = \text{SD}_o^m(x, 1, y_{-m}) R^m(x, p_m, p_{-m})$$

As in the single-output case, we may now derive an efficiency interpretation for output m, namely

$$\pounds_{om} = 1 - \epsilon_{C_m} \frac{1}{\text{SD}_o^m(x, y_m, y_{-m})} \frac{1}{\frac{R^m(x, p_m, p_{-m})}{C^m(y_m, y_{-m}, w)}}$$

where ϵ_{C_m} is the cost elasticity for output m. $\frac{1}{\text{SD}_o^m(x, y_m, y_{-m})}$ is the Farrell technical efficiency for m

and

$\frac{R^m(x, p_m, p_{-m})}{C^m(y_m, y_{-m}, w)}$ is its Georgescu-Roegen (1951) "return to the dollar".

Using the Färe and Karagiannis (2021) aggregation procedure, we have

$$\pounds_o^M = 1 - \sum_{m=1}^{M} s_m \epsilon_{C_m} \frac{1}{\text{SD}_o^m(x, y_m, y_{-m})} \frac{1}{\frac{R^m(x, p_m, p_{-m})}{C^m(y_m, y_{-m}, w)}}$$

4. Aggregation over Firms: Industry Indexes

Suppose there are $k = 1, \ldots, K$ firms producing and selling the same (single) good. Then, of course, we no longer have a monopoly market but rather an oligopolistic market.

We define the Lerner Index for an individual firm as

$$\pounds_{ok} = \frac{p^k - \frac{\partial C(y, w)}{\partial y^k}}{p^k}, \quad k = 1, \ldots, K$$

where the firms may have different price p^k, quantity of output y^k and cost functions C^k. Here we assume that they face the same input prices w for simplicity. Again following Färe and Karagiannis (2021), we may aggregate over firms by weighting them by shares, defined in this case as

$$s^k = \frac{p^k y^k}{\sum_{k=1}^{K} p^k y^k} \geq 0, \quad k = 1, \ldots, K$$

and

$$\sum_{k=1}^{K} s^k = 1$$

Thus, we have

$$\pounds_o^K = \sum_{k=1}^{K} s^k \pounds_{ok}$$

as our measure of the Lerner Index aggregated over firms with a single, homogeneous output.

For the case of multiple outputs y_m^k, $m = 1, \ldots, M$, firm $k's$ share of the good m is

$$s_m^k = \frac{p_m^k y_m^k}{\sum_{m=1}^{M} p_m^k y_m^k} \geq 0, \quad \sum_{k=1}^{K} s_m^k = 1$$

Then we may define the industry level Lerner Index for homogeneous output good m as

$$\pounds_{om}^K = \sum_{k=1}^{K} s_m^k \pounds_m^k$$

where

$$\pounds_{om}^k = \frac{p_m^k - \frac{\partial C(y,w)}{\partial y_m^k}}{p_m^k}, \quad m = 1, \ldots, M$$

is firm $k's$ Lerner Index for good m.

5. Estimating the Lerner Indexes

In general, we do not expect to observe marginal costs, instead we are more likely to observe data on costs, output and input prices which we can use to estimate the cost function and marginal costs. Typically, these would be estimated parametrically, requiring specification of an appropriate functional form. Given the properties of the cost function and underlying technology, we have shown elsewhere that the translog cost function with appropriate constraints on the parameters is suitable:

$$C(y, w) = \alpha_o + \sum_{m=1}^{M} \alpha_m \ln y_m + 1/2 \sum_{m=1}^{M} \sum_{m'=1}^{M} \alpha_{mm'} \ln y_m \ln y_{m'}$$

$$+ \sum_{n=1}^{N} \beta_n \ln w_n + 1/2 \sum_{n=1}^{N} \sum_{n'=1}^{N} \beta_{nn'} \ln w_n \ln w_{n'}$$

$$+ \sum_{m=1}^{M} \sum_{n=1}^{N} \gamma_{mn} \ln y_m \ln w_n \tag{4}$$

The parameters may be estimated using the deterministic frontier method of Aigner-Chu (1968) or as a stochastic frontier, see Kumbhakar and Lovell (2000).

If output prices are not observable, one may estimate shadow output prices. Recall that the profit function[3] may be defined as

$$\Pi(p, w) = \max_y py - \frac{wx}{D_i(y, x)}$$

where $D_i(y, x)$ is Shephard's (1953) input distance function:

$$D_i(y, x) = \max\{\lambda : x/\lambda \in L(y)\}$$

The first-order conditions from the profit maximization problem are

$$p_m = -\frac{wx}{D_i(y, x)^2} \frac{\partial D_i(y, x)}{\partial y_m}, \quad m = 1, \ldots, M$$

which yields the shadow price we seek for the Lerner Index, when price data are not available.

In order to estimate $p_m, m = 1, \ldots, M$, we require specification and estimation of the input distance function. Given the properties of the

---

[3] See Färe and Primont (1995).

distance function, again a translog parameterization is indicated, namely estimate

$$\ln D_i(y, x) = \alpha_o + \sum_{m=1}^{M} \alpha_m \ln y_m + 1/2 \sum_{m=1}^{M} \sum_{m'=1}^{M} \alpha_{mm'} \ln y_m \ln y_{m'}$$

$$+ \sum_{n=1}^{N} \beta_n \ln x_n + 1/2 \sum_{n=1}^{N} \sum_{n'=1}^{N} \beta_{nn'} \ln x_n \ln x_{n'}$$

$$+ \sum_{m=1}^{M} \sum_{n=1}^{N} \gamma_{mn} \ln y_m \ln x_n \tag{5}$$

again with the appropriate restrictions on the parameters. Frontier estimation is recommended; Aigner–Chu deterministic model (1968) or stochastic frontier following, e.g., Kumbhakar and Lovell (2000), are possible choices.

https://doi.org/10.1142/9789811285936_0003

Chapter 3

Monopsony Power: Input Lerner Indexes[*]

Rolf G. Färe[†], Shawna Grosskopf[†], and Dimitris Margaritis[‡]

†Oregon State University, Corvallis, USA
‡University of Auckland, Auckland, New Zealand

1. Introduction

In this chapter, we turn to market power in input markets, beginning with the single-input case. We derive an economic efficiency interpretation with associated decompositions. We generalize our input index to the multiple input case which introduces the issue of aggregation both across inputs and firms. We conclude with possible estimation strategies.

2. The Single-Input Case

In this section, we develop a Lerner-type index to capture deviations from competitive behavior in input markets. For concreteness we refer to labor markets, thus focusing on monopsonistic behavior. We begin with a single firm, the monopsonist, employing a single input, x, to produce output quantities $y \in \Re_+^M$.

Given output prices $p \in \Re_+^M$ the revenue function for our monopsonist is defined as

$$R(x, p) = \max_y \{py : y \in P(x)\} \tag{1}$$

---

[*]We thank Vic Tremblay for his helpful comments.

We model technology by its output sets

$$P(x) = \{y : x \text{ can produce } y\}, x \in \Re_+ \tag{2}$$

in the single input case, $N = 1$.

We impose the standard regularity conditions, see Färe and Primont (1995) for details.

Next, we consider the profit maximization problem in terms of the revenue function

$$\max_x R(x, p) - wx$$

The first-order or equilibrium condition is

$$\partial R(x, p) - w = 0$$

In parallel to the output-oriented Lerner Index, we define a single input-oriented Lerner Index, or measure of monopsony power as the normalized deviation derived from the first order condition:

$$\pounds_i = \frac{\frac{\partial R(x,p)}{\partial x} - w}{w} \tag{3}$$

We could have also defined it as

$$\frac{w - \frac{\partial R(x,p)}{\partial x}}{w}$$

but here we choose the former, which can be derived from the Nerlovian profit indicator $\aleph$. Recall that $\aleph$ is defined as

$$\aleph = \frac{\Pi(p, w) - \Pi^o}{pg_y + wg_x}$$

where $\Pi(p, w)$ is the profit function, Π^o is the observed profit and g_y, g_x are the directional vectors. If we set $g_y = 0$ and $g_x = 1$, we may write the indicator as the maximization problem

$$\aleph = \max_x \frac{R(x, p) - wx - \Pi^o}{w}$$

Its first-order condition may be written as the input-oriented Lerner monopsony index, namely

$$\pounds_i = \frac{\frac{\partial R(x,p)}{\partial x} - w}{w}$$

Following Ashenfelter *et al.* (2010, p. 205), one can show that this input-based index, like its output-based counterpart, can be given an elasticity interpretation

$$\pounds_i = \frac{\frac{\partial R(x,p)}{dx} - w}{w} = \frac{1}{\epsilon_w} \tag{4}$$

where ϵ_w is the wage elasticity of labor.

Earlier, we showed that Chambers *et al.* (2014) provided an economic efficiency interpretation of the Lerner monopoly index. Here we develop the analog for the monopsony index. To that end, we return to some underlying production theoretic concepts. We begin with the input requirement set

$$L(y) = \{x : x \text{ can produce } y\}$$

which is used to define Shephard's input distance function

$$D_i(y, x) = \min \left\{ \lambda : \frac{x}{\lambda} \in L(y) \right\}$$

The associated dual cost function is

$$C(y, w) = \min_x \{wx : x \in L(y)\}$$
$$= \min_x \{wx : D_i(y, x) \geqq 1\} \tag{5}$$

since the input distance function satisfies representation, i.e., given weak disposability of inputs, it completely represents the input set

$$L(y) = \{x : D_i(y, x) \geqq 1\}$$

From duality theory, see Färe and Primont (1995), it follows that

$$wx = D_i(y, x)C(y, w)$$

and since the distance function is homogeneous of degree $+1$ in inputs, we have

$$wx = xD_i(y, 1)C(y, w)$$

thus

$$w = D_i(y, 1)C(y, w)$$

We may now write the monopsony index and derive a three-component efficiency decomposition as

$$
\begin{aligned}
\pounds_i &= \frac{\frac{\partial R(x,p)}{\partial x} - w}{w} \\
&= \frac{\partial R(x, p)}{\partial x} - 1 \\
&= \frac{\partial R(x, p)}{\partial x} \frac{xR(x, p)}{xR(x, p)D_i(y, 1)C(y, w)} - 1 \\
&= \epsilon_R \frac{1}{D_i(y, x)\frac{C(y,w)}{R(x,p)}} - 1
\end{aligned}
\tag{6}
$$

i.e., the index can be decomposed into three factors (minus one), namely

revenue elasticity ϵ_R

Farrell input technical efficiency $\dfrac{1}{D_i(y, x)}$

"return to the dollar" $\dfrac{R(x, p)}{C(y, w)}$

where the third component is due to Georgescu-Roegen (1951). The first component can tell us about scale properties of the technology, Farrell technical efficiency identifies deviations from efficiency due to non-optimal employment of inputs relative to best practice and return to the dollar is a measure of profitability.

As we showed with the monopoly index under CRS, the monopsony index can also be expressed in terms of Farrell efficiency, here as an input-oriented measure.

Note that under CRS, the revenue function is homogeneous of degree $+1$ in inputs. Thus, for the single input case, we have

$$R(x, p) = x R(1, p)$$

This implies that the revenue elasticity takes the value one,

$$\epsilon_R = 1$$

In addition under CRS, maximum profit is zero and hence we have

$$\frac{R(x, p)}{C(y, w)} = 1$$

We can now conclude that

$$£_i = \frac{1}{D_i(y, x)} - 1$$

And with technical efficiency, we have $£_i = 0$, i.e., no market power.

3. Lerner Input Indexes and Their Aggregations

As we did for the output indexes previously, we now generalize our single-input index to the multiple input case, i.e., $x \in \Re_+^N$. The key is to use partial derivatives. The $n = 1, \ldots, N$ input Lerner Index is

$$£_{in} = \frac{\frac{\partial R(x,p)}{\partial x_n} - w_n}{w_n}, \quad n = 1, \ldots, N.$$

As with the single-input case, these individual input indexes measure the deviation between the profit maximizing equilibrium derived from

$$\max_x R(x, p) - wx$$

which yields

$$\partial R(x, p) - w_n = 0, \quad n = 1, \ldots, N$$

Again following the structure of the previous section, we next develop an elasticity interpretation of this index. Recall the Nerlovian multi-input profit indicator may be written as

$$\aleph = \frac{\Pi(p, w) - \Pi^o}{pg_y + wg_x}$$

where g_y, g_x are the directional vectors. Letting $g_x \in \Re_+^N$, $g_x \neq 0$, we may now write the indicator as

$$\aleph = \max_{x_1, \ldots, x_N} \frac{R(x, p) - \sum_{n=1}^{N} w_n x_n - \Pi^o}{pg_y + \sum_{n=1}^{N} w_n g_{x_n}}$$

If we choose $g_{n_i} = 0$, for $i = 1, \ldots, N$ except for g_n as well as setting $g_y = 0$, the first-order condition with respect to n is

$$\frac{\frac{\partial R(x,p)}{\partial x_n} - w_n}{w_n}, \quad n = 1, \ldots, N$$

which is the Lerner monopsony index for individual input n.

In order to aggregate the individual input indexes over all n, we apply the generalized denominator rule developed by Färe and Karagiannis (2021). They suggest using a share-weighted index, where

$$s_n = \frac{w_n x_n}{\sum_{n=1}^{N} w_n x_n} \geq 0 \quad \text{and} \quad \sum_{n=1}^{N} s_n = 1$$

are the appropriate weights. Our aggregate monopsony index may then be written as

$$\begin{aligned}
\pounds_i^N &= \sum_{n=1}^{N} s_n \left(\frac{\frac{\partial R(x,p)}{\partial x_n} - w_n}{w_n} \right) \\
&= \sum_{n=1}^{N} s_n \pounds_{in}
\end{aligned} \tag{7}$$

4.   Lerner Industry Indexes: Aggregation over Firms

Suppose we observe $k = 1, \ldots, K$ firms in an industry using and hiring the same single input. In this case, we may speak of an oligopsonist rather than monopsonist.

Let firm $k's$ Lerner monopsony index equal

$$\pounds_{ik} = \frac{\frac{\partial R(x,p)}{\partial x^k} - w^k}{w^k}, \quad k = 1, \ldots, K$$

where the firms may have different input price, different input quantity as well as different revenue functions. They may but need not face the dame output prices p.

Employing the Färe and Karagiannis (2021) share-weighted model, we may aggregate over firms to obtain the industry index. The shares are defined as

$$s^k = \frac{w^k x^k}{\sum_{k=1}^{K} w^k x^k} \geq 0, \quad \text{with} \quad \sum_{k=1}^{K} s^k = 1$$

Then the aggregate index for input n is defined as

$$\pounds_{in}^{K} = \sum_{k=1}^{K} s_n^k \pounds_n^k$$

where

$$\pounds_{in}^{k} = \frac{\frac{\partial R(x,p)}{\partial x_n^k} - w_n^k}{w_n^k}, \quad n = 1, \ldots, N$$

is firm $k's$ monopsony index for input n.

5. Estimating the Lerner Input Indexes

In this section, we provide models for estimating the Lerner input/ monopsony index, which parallels that developed earlier for the monopoly case. Our monopsony indexes developed above are specified in terms of marginal revenue as well as input prices. Since we do not generally observe marginal revenue, we instead start with estimation of the parent revenue function and take the appropriate derivatives based on those estimates. In specifying the revenue function, we seek a parametric functional form consistent with the underlying properties of the revenue function as well as allowing for differentiability and flexibility. Since the revenue function is homogeneous in output prices, we favour the translog form[1]:

$$\ln R(x, p) = \alpha_o + \sum_{n=1}^{N} \alpha_n x_n + 1/2 \sum_{n=1}^{N} \sum_{n'=1}^{N} \alpha_{nn'} \ln x_n \ln x_{n'}$$

$$+ \sum_{m=1}^{M} \beta_m \ln p_m + \sum_{m=1}^{M} \sum_{m'=1}^{M} \beta_{mm'} \ln p_m \ln p_{m'}$$

$$+ \sum_{n=1}^{N} \sum_{m=1}^{M} \gamma_{nm} \ln x_n \ln p_m \tag{8}$$

with the appropriate constraints on the parameters. The parameters of the function may be estimated using the (deterministic) Aigner-Chu (1968) approach based on linear programming, or a stochastic frontier approach, see Kumbhakar and Lovell (2000). In the latter case, specification of a composed error term would also be included.

If input prices are not observed, they may be estimated as well, yielding shadow prices. These can be obtained as first-order conditions of the profit maximization problem:

$$\Pi(p, w) = \max_x p \frac{y}{D_o(x, y)} - wx$$

where $D_o(x, y)$ is Shephard's (1970) output distance function

$$D_o(x, y) = \inf\{\theta : y/\theta \in P(x)\}$$

The first-order conditions yield

$$w_n = \frac{py}{D_o(x, y)^2} \frac{\partial D_o(x, y)}{\partial x_n}, \quad n = 1, \dots, N$$

Since the output distance function is homogeneous in output quantities, the translog functional form is preferred.

---

[1] If the data set is not riddled with zeros.

Part B

Lerner Indexes: Contributed Chapters

https://doi.org/10.1142/9789811285936_0004

Chapter 4

Estimating Monopsony Power Using Revenue and Distance Functions

**Rolf G. Färe*, Shawna Grosskopf*, Maryam Hasannasab[†],
and Dimitris Margaritis[†]**

*Oregon State University, Corvallis, USA
†University of Auckland, Auckland, New Zealand

1. Introduction

The study of monopsony power has come under increasing scrutiny in both academic and policy circles in recent years. At the 2018 Central Bankers' annual meeting in Jackson Hole, Wyoming, much discussion focussed on the effects of market power in labor markets, evident from sluggish overall wage growth despite record low unemployment in the post-crisis period. Monopsony power, in part associated with the rise of economically powerful 'superstar' firms in the US with high markups and a low labor share of value-added, also drew much attention within the Obama administration as a potential explanation of dismal wage growth and falling share of national income going to labor despite the longest economic expansion in history (see Autor *et al.*, 2019; Weil, 2018).

Monopsony power does not specifically apply to the labor market, even if it has been the focus of much work in economics, notably Robinson (1969), Manning (2003), Ashenfelter *et al.* (2010) and Card and Krueger (2015), among others. With interest rates hovering around zero during the pandemic crisis and previously during the Global Financial Crisis, questions arose about the effects of monopsony power by banks in the market for customer deposits and hence on earnings inequality much to the detriment of those living off fixed incomes.[1] More recently, questions arise in relation to monopsony power by banks in the deposits markets following increases in interest rates by central banks. As shown by Drechsler *et al.* (2017), cash becomes more expensive to hold when central banks hike key policy interest rates, allowing banks with market power to raise deposit spreads without losing deposits to cash, albeit the increase in spreads may trigger large deposit outflows. The contraction of deposits will reduce bank lending. This is important since the deposits channel is likely to affect the supply of other liquid assets in the market and raise the liquidity premium and hence the cost of capital. There is also much other evidence pointing in the direction of an incomplete pass-through from interest rates determined in competitive markets for securities and other debt instruments to retail interest rates in banking markets. For example, Neumark and Sharpe (1992), Sharpe (1997), Kahn *et al.* (1999), Rosen (2007) and Kopecky and Van Hoose (2012), among others, argue that imperfect competition is a key feature of the incomplete pass-through between market interest rates and bank retail interest rates.

But very low interest rates pose a risk to financial stability since they may adversely impact bank profitability, especially for banks that rely more on deposits for their funding (Heider *et al.*, 2019). And banks that pay higher deposit rates may be more eager to invest in risky assets (Arping, 2017). For example, more bank competition erodes market power, reduces franchise value and encourages risk-taking behavior (Berger *et al.*, 2009). This in turn raises the issue of efficiency since we would expect more efficient banks to be in a better position to offset adverse credit shocks.[2] The purpose of this study is to introduce an integrative framework to study firm efficiency and market structure, with a focus on measuring banks' pricing power in the market for deposits.

---

[1] Income distribution considerations have played a key role in shaping competition policies in financial markets. For example, more competition among banks (e.g., removing restrictions on intrastate branching) in the US was shown to be associated with a reduction in income inequality (Beck *et al.*, 2010).

[2] While more efficient banks potentially have more capacity for riskier behavior, they may choose less risky portfolios to protect franchise value in more concentrated markets. Similarly, banks with more market power may take on lower risk and have a lower probability of default (Agoraki *et al.*, 2011).

Three approaches have dominated the literature on bank competition: market structure and associated indicators such as the number of banks in the industry and concentration indexes; regulatory indicators that measure the contestability of the banking sector by considering the degree of entry and exit in the markets to discern the degree of competition; and more formal competition measures based on the 'new empirical industrial organization' literature that study bank pricing behavior in terms of marginal revenue, marginal cost and cost pricing pass-through (Degryse *et al.*, 2014). The first approach encompasses the contrasting effects of the structure conduct-performance hypothesis (Mason, 1939; Bain, 1956) where higher profits relate to the ability of banks to exercise market power in concentrated markets (Berger and Hannan, 1998),[3] and the efficient-structure (ES) hypothesis under which higher profits and market concentration relate to firm efficiency (Demsetz, 1973).[4] Alternatively, market power may result in higher costs (rather than higher profits) due to inefficiencies, as the management is under less pressure to minimize costs — the so-called "quiet life effect" (Berger and Hannan, 1998). The second approach suggests that competitive behavior can exist in concentrated markets if firms are vulnerable to hit-and-run entry; in other words, when markets are contestable (Baumol *et al.*, 1982). Our measure of market power draws on the third approach that measures competitive conduct directly rather than inferring it through an analysis of market structure. Specifically, we focus on the Lerner Index, a bank-specific measure of market power based on price markups over marginal costs (Lerner, 1934). In contrast, the Rosse–Panzar H-statistic provides an aggregate measure of competition based on the sum of elasticities of firm revenue with respect to input prices (Rosse and Panzar, 1977).

While several studies estimate the Lerner Index using production technologies, typically constructed parametrically using translog functions,[5] this is to our knowledge the first attempt to offer a theoretical framework for

---

[3] Berger and Hannan (1998) examine the relationship between concentration and deposit interest rates after the deregulation of the US market in the 1980s and find lower interest rates in more concentrated markets.

[4] Berger and Hannan (1998) find support for the hypothesis that market concentration is associated with lower bank efficiency, a contradiction of the efficient-structure hypothesis.

[5] See Berger *et al.* (2009), Agoraki *et al.* (2011), among others.

the study of monopsony power encompassing complete characterizations of technology in the form of distance functions in the quantity space and their value duals, the revenue and profit functions. In addition, we show how to aggregate individual Lerner indices into an overall index of market power using the Denominator Rule of Färe and Karagiannis (2017).

Following the theory part presented in Section 2, we apply our version of the Lerner Index to measure monopsony power in the market for bank deposits in Section 3. Section 4 concludes this chapter.

2. The Theory

In this section, we develop a Lerner-type index to capture deviations from competitive behavior in input markets, thus focusing on monopsonistic behavior. We show how this index may be estimated using distance functions which are measures of firm efficiency; data requirements include input and output quantities and output prices. Hence, we adopt an integrative approach to the measurement of both firm efficiency and market power. If input prices are available, monopsony power is measured by the difference between the input price and the marginal revenue with respect to a change in the input. We are also thinking of input prices as unknowns for which we may solve. This may be relevant in situations where input prices are not available or reliable.

In terms of notation, let $y \in \Re_+^M$ denote output quantities and $x \in \Re_+^N$ input quantities. We model technology by its output sets

$$P(x) = \{y : x \text{ can produce } y\}, \quad x \in \Re_+^N \tag{1}$$

We impose the standard regularity conditions, see Färe and Primont (1995) for details.

Given output prices $p \in \Re_+^M$ the revenue function is defined as

$$R(x, p) = \max_y \{py : y \in P(x)\} \tag{2}$$

By its definition, this function is homogeneous in prices, i.e.,

$$R(x, \lambda p) = \lambda R(x, p), \quad \lambda > 0 \tag{3}$$

In addition, under convexity, it is the dual representation of technology:

$$P(x) = \{y : py \leqq R(x, p), \ p \in \Re_+^M\} \tag{4}$$

A second representation of the output sets is the Shephard (1970) output distance function

$$D_o(x, y) = \inf_\theta \{\theta : (y/\theta) \in P(x)\} \tag{5}$$

This function is homogeneous in the scaled output vector y,

$$D_o(x, \lambda y) = \lambda D_o(x, y), \quad \lambda > 0 \tag{6}$$

and under weak disposability of outputs[6] it is also a complete representation of the technology, see Färe and Primont (1995) for proof,

$$P(x) = \{y : D_o(x, y) \leqq 1\}, \quad x \in \Re_+^N \tag{7}$$

Since we are interested in measuring monopsony power, we introduce what could be called an 'input-oriented' Lerner-type index. We begin with the single-input case, say labor, and define

$$\pounds = \frac{w - \partial R(x, p)/\partial x}{w} \tag{8}$$

which is the ratio of the difference between the input price $w >= 0$ and the marginal revenue with respect to a change in input x,[7] relative to the wage. Values of $\pounds < 0$ signal evidence of deviations from competitive labor market behavior, i.e., monopsony. As a reference, recall that the standard textbook definition of the Lerner Index in terms of output price is[8]

$$\pounds = \frac{p - \partial C(y, w)/\partial y}{p} \tag{9}$$

For the single-output case, this is the ratio of the difference between output price and marginal cost of output, to the price of output, where $\pounds > 0$ signals

---

[6]$P(x)$ satisfies weak disposability of outputs if $y \in P(x)$ and $0 \leq \theta \leq 1$ concludes $\theta y \in P(x)$.

[7]This may be thought of as the difference between the wage rate and marginal revenue product of labor. Note that (8) is also the (negative) inverse of the labor supply curve, hence monopsony power can be exercised by any firm facing an upward sloping labor supply curve (see Ashenfelter *et al.*, 2010).

[8]Lerner (1934).

deviations from perfect competition (monopoly power). The monopoly and monopsony indexes are thus symmetric.[9]

Given a revenue function $R(x, p)$ which we presently show how to specify and estimate marginal revenue $\partial R(x, p)/\partial x$ with respect to input quantity is straightforward to derive. If the input price is unknown, we require some additional effort to identify it.

Recall that the profit function is defined as

$$\Pi(w, p) = \max_{x,y} py - wx \quad \text{s.t. } (x, y) \in T \tag{10}$$

where

$$T = \{(x, y) : x \text{ can produce } y\}, \quad \text{or} \quad T = \{(x, y) : y \in P(x)\} \tag{11}$$

Thus we may write

$$\Pi(w, x) = \max_{x,y} py - wx \quad \text{s.t. } y \in P(x) \tag{12}$$

And from (7) we know that the output distance function is a representation of the output sets $P(x)$ so we have

$$\Pi(w, x) = \max_{x,y} py - wx \quad \text{s.t. } D_o(x, y) - .7ex \leqq 1 \tag{13}$$

This is of course a constrained optimization problem, generally solved using Lagrangian techniques. However, Färe and Primont (1995) show that this problem can be transformed into an unconstrained optimization problem, namely

$$\Pi(w, x) = \max_{x,y} p \frac{y}{D_o(x, y)} - wx \tag{14}$$

The first-order condition with respect to (single) input x is

$$-\frac{py}{(D_o(x, y))^2} \partial D_o(x, y)/\partial x - w = 0 \tag{15}$$

or equivalently, we can solve for the shadow price of input x as

$$w = -\frac{py}{(D_o(x, y))^2} \partial D_o(x, y)/\partial x \tag{16}$$

---

[9]The monopsony (monopoly) index may be generalized to the case of multiple inputs (outputs).

which can be used to compute the Lerner monopsony index when input prices are not available or not reliable.

We may now consider the case in which input x is a vector. In this case, we may define individual input monopsony indexes as

$$\pounds_n = \frac{w_n - \partial R(x, p)/\partial x_n}{w_n}, \quad n = 1, \ldots, N \tag{17}$$

We may aggregate these into an overall index using what has been called the Denominator Rule, Färe and Karagiannis (2017):

$$\pounds = \sum_{n=1}^{N} s_n \frac{w_n - \partial R(x, p)/\partial x_n}{w_n} \tag{18}$$

where the shares s_n are value weights which may be specified as

$$s_n = \frac{w_n}{\sum_{n=1}^{N} w_n} \tag{19}$$

Returning to the single input index, we may set

$$w = \partial R(x, p)/\partial x = \text{MR} \tag{20}$$

and compute the optimal input quantity for the shadow price w. As an example take

$$R(x, p) = x^2 R(1, p) \tag{21}$$

then

$$\partial R(x, p)/\partial x = 2x R(1, p) \tag{22}$$

and using $w = \text{MR}$ yields

$$w = 2x R(1, p) \tag{23}$$

and the optimal input quantity is

$$x = w/2R(1, p) \tag{24}$$

In the case in which x is a vector, we have $n = 1, \ldots, N$ equations to solve.

To execute our theory, we need to parameterize and estimate the distance and revenue functions. We assume that our functions should be flexible, i.e., generalized quadratic:

$$f(q) = \rho^{-1}\left(a_o + \sum_{i=1}^{I} a_i g(q_i) + \sum_{i=1}^{I}\sum_{j=1}^{J} a_{ij} g(q_i)g(q_j)\right) \qquad (25)$$

where

$$f : \Re^I \to \Re, \; g : \Re \to \Re, \; \rho^{-1} : \Re \to \Re \qquad (26)$$

Färe and Sung (1986) show that if this function is homogeneous, like the distance and revenue functions, the resulting functional equation has two solutions, namely the translog form:

$$f(q) = a_o + \sum_{i=1}^{I} a_i \ln q_i + \sum_{i=1}^{I}\sum_{j=1}^{J} a_{ij}\ln q_i \ln q_j \qquad (27)$$

and the mean of order ρ:

$$f(q) = \left(\sum_{i=1}^{I}\sum_{j=1}^{J} a_{ij} q_i^{\rho/2} q_j^{\rho/2}\right)^{1/\rho} \qquad (28)$$

Since the latter has only second-order parameters a_{ij} while the translog has both first-order a_i and second-order a_{ij} parameters, barring data riddled with zeros, our preferred choice of functional form is the translog.

3. Empirical Application

We use data obtained from Orbis Bank Focus during the period 2013–2016 to estimate the Lerner Index for bank deposits in Central and Eastern Europe (CEE) countries. Since most of the CEE banking systems are highly concentrated (see Table 1), it is of interest to study the performance of banks in these markets in the post-crisis environment, and the linkages between market power and bank performance.[10] We follow the intermediation

[10]Studies on bank efficiency and market competition in CEE countries include Fries and Taci (2005), Koutsomanoli-Filippaki *et al.* (2009a, 2009b) and Yildirim and Philippatos (2007), among others. One interesting observation about CEE banking is that foreign entry which in many cases was quite

Table 1. Descriptive Statistics

Variables				Mean (Std. Dev.)				
	CZ	EE	HU	LT	LV	PL	SK	All
FA	0.052	0.004	0.132	0.016	0.025	0.092	0.051	0.062
	(0.116)	(0.003)	(0.213)	(0.021)	(0.020)	(0.141)	(0.057)	(0.122)
DEP	4.691	0.834	5.833	2.214	1.431	8.680	3.975	4.940
	(7.055)	(1.241)	(7.277)	(2.173)	(1.295)	(10.756)	(3.535)	(7.590)
EQ	0.744	0.211	0.935	0.364	0.216	1.416	0.560	0.790
	(1.102)	(0.350)	(1.301)	(0.383)	(0.277)	(1.791)	(0.533)	(1.255)
EMP	0.052	0.010	0.125	0.022	0.020	0.131	0.052	0.072
	(0.086)	(0.013)	(0.191)	(0.017)	(0.015)	(0.153)	(0.047)	(0.119)
OBF	1.613	0.243	1.579	0.388	0.236	1.841	0.725	1.205
	(2.573)	(0.375)	(1.098)	(0.539)	(0.363)	(2.047)	(0.851)	(1.838)
P_OEA	0.022	0.061	0.051	0.020	0.014	0.037	0.027	0.030
	(0.016)	(0.182)	(0.027)	(0.010)	(0.010)	(0.021)	(0.009)	(0.048)
P_LN	0.049	0.035	0.067	0.046	0.056	0.054	0.051	0.053
	(0.022)	(0.013)	(0.022)	(0.038)	(0.021)	(0.021)	(0.016)	(0.023)
*P(NII)	0.008	0.014	0.023	0.015	0.026	0.013	0.008	0.015
	(0.009)	(0.010)	(0.007)	(0.013)	(0.022)	(0.009)	(0.003)	(0.013)
P_DEP	0.014	0.005	0.024	0.008	0.008	0.021	0.012	0.012
	0.008	0.003	0.014	0.004	0.005	0.009	0.006	0.010
R_EFF	0.850	0.707	0.805	0.768	0.717	0.783	0.867	0.796
	(0.184)	(0.106)	(0.149)	(0.115)	(0.151)	(0.169)	(0.117)	(0.165)
LI	−1.442	−2.402	0.387	−1.137	−1.946	−1.258	−0.246	−1.180
	(6.601)	(1.821)	(0.635)	(1.307)	(2.210)	(5.570)	(0.660)	(4.520)
# OBS	83	20	35	20	53	94	41	346
	0.026	−1.922	0.387	−1.137	−1.124	0.253	−0.246	−0.249
LI_W	(0.846)	(1.125)	(0.635)	(1.307)	(1.034)	(0.751)	(0.660)	(1.083)
# OBS_W	76	18	35	20	44	86	41	320

Notes: CZ = Czech Republic; EE = Estonia; HU = Hungary; LT = Lithuania; LV = Latvia; PL = Poland; SK = Slovak Republic. Bank inputs are fixed assets (FA), deposits (DEP), equity capital (EQ), employee expenses (EMP) and other borrowed funds (OBF), all measured in billions of Euros. Bank output prices are P_OEA price of other earning assets, P_LN price of loans and P_NII price of non-interest income activities. P_DEP is the price of deposits, R_EFF is revenue efficiency and LI is the Learner index (LI_W are Lerner Index averages with some outliers, large negative values, removed).

dominant through acquisitions or exit of local banks did not increase competition among banks in CEE countries. Whether foreign entry improves bank efficiency through superior management and lending technologies of the new entrants and through positive spillovers to their local competitors is generally an open question albeit much early evidence from the CEE region, e.g., Bonin *et al.* (2005), Fries and Taci (2005), Koutsomanoli-Philippaki *et al.* (2009a) and Havrylchyk and Jurzyk (2011) point in this direction.

approach (see Sealey and Lindley, 1977) to model the production of bank services.

We assume banks use a production technology consisting of five inputs: staff costs, fixed assets, deposits, equity and other borrowed funds, and three outputs: loans, other earning assets and non-interest income. Since we estimate a revenue function, we require output prices. We measure the price of loans as interest income on loans over total loans, the price of other earning assets as interest income on other earning assets over other earning assets, and the price of non-interest income earning activities as non-interest income over total loans and deposits.

Revenue efficiency is estimated using a translog function where bank revenue is modeled as a function of bank inputs and output prices. We use the Aigner and Chu (1968) method to estimate the parameters of the translog model by minimizing the sum of deviations of the revenue function value from the revenue frontier subject to the underlying technology constraints. The constraint conditions cover the feasibility, monotonicity and homogeneity properties of the revenue function. Equity capital is a quasi-fixed input, so it is fixed in the short run but variable in the long run, and its shadow price is not constrained to be positive recognizing that negative shadow prices may prevail at least temporarily during periods of extensive deleveraging and de-risking as was the case in CEE banking at the aftermath of the global financial crisis.[11] Since we are interested in measuring monopsony power for deposits, we apply the 'input-oriented' Lerner-type index given by (8) to measure market power where the price of deposits is measured as the ratio of interest paid on deposits over total deposits.

Table 1 presents the descriptive statistics of the data as well as bank performance (revenue efficiency) measures and Lerner indices (LI) of monopsony power. Revenue efficiency is highest in the Slovak and Czech

---

[11] Such deleveraging was more pronounced for subsidiaries of a parent bank operating in another country (EBRD, 2015). The financial crisis had a significant impact on CEE banks many of which were foreign owned, adversely affecting both the funding and lending sides of their balance sheet. Prior to the crisis, cross-border capital flows played a key role in driving strong GDP growth in the CEE region. Following the crisis, net capital flows from Western Europe fell dramatically as the Eurozone experienced a protracted recession, with cross-border lending and investment declining rapidly, thereby transmitting the crisis to the CEE region (EBRD, 2015).

Republics and lowest in Estonia and Latvia which also have the least competitive markets for deposits as indicated by the estimated value of the Lerner Index. Hungary is the most competitive market for deposits. Removing the effect of some outliers (large negative Lerner Index values) we find that the market for deposits is also competitive in the Czech Republic and Poland. These results are reported at the bottom of the table (see row labeled LI-W). Note that these outliers have a particularly marked effect on the variance of the LI statistic for the Czech Republic and Poland.

Table 2 reports various bank performance measures across five quantiles of the Lerner Index distribution. We find that larger banks (column 1) pay more competitive deposits. Profitability measured by return on assets (column 2) and return on equity (column 3) are higher while loan loss provisions to equity ratios (column 6), a measure of bank risk, are lower in market segments with more monopsony power in deposits.[12] Similarly, higher monopsony pricing power is associated with more operationally cost efficient (column 5), more liquid banks (column 7), those who are better capitalized, i.e., have more equity in relation to loans (column 8), and are more diversified (column 10). In contrast, more traditional banks with higher loan-to-assets ratios (column 9) pay more competitive deposits.

We turn next to study determinants of market power and bank performance in the multivariate context using fixed effects panel regressions. Table 3 provides information on bank characteristics that may be associated with market power (columns 1 and 2) and bank characteristics that may be associated with bank profitability (columns 3 and 4). We find that the relationship between monopsony power and our measure of firm performance (revenue efficiency) is non-monotonic portrayed via an inverted U-shaped curve. This is consistent with similar findings (e.g., see Aghion *et al.*, 2005) in the literature underpinning the relationship between competition and firm performance.[13]

Since both the Lerner Index and revenue efficiency estimates are obtained from the same model, there is an issue of endogeneity, which

---

[12] Similarly, Agoraki *et al.* (2011) report that CEE banks with market power tend to take on lower credit risk and have a lower probability of default.

[13] Evidence on the relationship between competition and efficiency in banking is largely mixed underpinned by arguments that either favor a positive relationship (Berger and Hannan, 1998) or a negative relationship (Demsetz, 1973).

Table 2. Descriptive Statistics

LI	TA	REFF	ROA	ROE	C_INC	LLP_EQ	LQA_TA	EQ_LN	LN_TA	NIL_R
					Mean (Std. Dev.)					
Q1	2.10 (2.491)	0.80 (0.18)	0.78 (1.30)	9.02 (19.83)	64.97 (25.43)	5.59 (10.58)	31.10 (23.19)	31.89 (24.39)	52.01 (28.63)	4749 (23.24)
Q2	5.71 (8.33)	0.79 (0.15)	0.65 (1.19)	6.39 (14.32)	64.56 (19.79)	5.92 (9.30)	22.63 (14.74)	21.99 (14.84)	53.47 (19.58)	42.56 (17.56)
Q3	5.46 (8.74)	0.76 (0.18)	0.54 (0.92)	4.90 (9.58)	67.35 (29.30)	6.24 (10.00)	20.40 (18.23)	21.38 (10.97)	54.97 (18.16)	34.53 (18.47)
Q4	8.36 (9.95)	0.81 (0.17)	0.40 (1.77)	3.37 (21.04)	60.49 (19.85)	9.23 (15.06)	14.53 (14.45)	18.88 (13.80)	60.50 (17.38)	34.25 (14.62)
Q5	14.34 (15.10)	0.82 (0.14)	0.48 (1.80)	3.55 (19.61)	58.37 (22.72)	10.02 (15.23)	14.68 (13.18)	17.09 (7.63)	62.56 (16.61)	35.92 (14.42)
All	7.19 (10.55)	0.80 (0.16)	0.57 (1.43)	5.44 (17.43)	63.16 (23.80)	7.42 (12.44)	20.67 (18.11)	22.24 (16.13)	56.70 (20.83)	38.94 (18.60)

Notes: LI is the Learner index, TA is total asset measured in billions of Euros, ROA is return on assets (%), ROE is return on equity (%), C_INC is total operating cost to interest income ratio (%), REFF is revenue efficiency, LLP_EQ is loan loss provisions to equity capital ratio (%), LQA_TA is liquid assets to total assets ratio (%), EQ_LN is equity to loans ratio (%), LN_TA is loans to total assets ratio (%) and NIL_R is non-interest income to revenue ratio (%).

Table 3. Panel Estimation.

Variables	Lerner Index Coeff.	Lerner Index t-Stats.	Lerner Index Coeff.	Lerner Index t-Stats.	ROA Coeff.	ROA t-Stats.	ROA Coeff.	ROA t-Stats.
$R.EFF$	0.3373**	2.0940	0.3365**	2.1574	0.0645**	2.0038	0.0675**	2.0531
$R.EFF^2$	-0.0025**	-2.1877	-0.0024**	0.0229	-0.004*	-1.9222	-0.0004***	-2.0087
LI					-0.0996**	-2.3339	-0.0969**	-2.3039
LI^2					-0.0020**	-2.3302	-0.0019**	-2.3010
SF_EA	-0.0341**	-2.8934						
NPL_LN	0.0468**	2.0449	0.0004*	1.7400				
$\log(TA)$	-1.5457*	-1.9428	-1.3329*	-1.7680	0.7130**	2.1776	0.7572**	2.2843
DEP_TA	0.0563**	2.1887						
LN_TA					-0.0436**	-2.4773	-0.0393**	-2.1875
EQ_TA					0.1270***	2.9430	0.0012***	2.9044
NII_R							0.0089	1.3758
Const	9.9389*	0.7393	7.3184*	0.7144	-11.3210**	-2.0210	-12.5940**	-2.1882
Adj R^2	0.5716		0.0.5678		0.7510		0.7524	

Notes: Fixed effects regression with robust standard errors. Lerner Index (LI) is the dependent variable in the first and second columns. Return on assets (ROA) is the dependent variable in the third and fourth columns. R.EFF is revenue efficiency, SF_FA is a stable funding measure, calculated as the ratio of customer deposits, long-term wholesale funding and equity over total earning assets, NPL_LN is non-performing (impaired loans) over total loans, TA is total assets, DEP_TA is deposits to total assets ratio, LN_TA is loans to total assets ratio, EQ_TA is equity capital to total assets ratio and NII_R is non-interest income to operating revenue ratio. *, ** and *** indicate significance at 10%, 5% and 1%, respectively.

fixed effects estimation can address only to the extent that unobserved bank heterogeneity is time invariant.[14] We also find that riskier banks with higher impaired to total loan ratios and banks with larger deposit-to-assets ratios, i.e., those that rely more on deposits to fund their assets, offer more competitive deposit rates, whereas banks that are larger and those that rely more on stable funding exercise more power in the market for deposits.

The last two columns of Table 3 show that the Lerner Index is negatively related to the return on assets. This finding is consistent with the predictions of the structure — conduct — performance hypothesis where higher profits reflect the ability of banks to exercise market power in concentrated markets. We find an inverted U-shape relationship between our measure of bank efficiency and bank profitability. We also find that larger banks, those that are better capitalized and more diversified appear to be more profitable.

4. Concluding Remarks

We have introduced an integrative framework to study firm efficiency and market structure. Specifically, we used distance functions to develop a Lerner-type index capturing deviations from competitive behavior in input markets. We have shown how this index may be estimated using information on input and output quantities and output prices.

While monopsony models have largely been developed for the labor market, they are also useful to study imperfect competition in other markets where firms may have price-setting power in input markets, even in the presence of many competitors, due to imperfect information (perhaps from search frictions) or high levels of input (e.g., job) differentiation as in the dynamic models of monopsony (see Manning, 2003, among others). In this sense, the study of retail deposits where search costs (e.g., moving accounts from one bank to another) may be significant, as also other forms of imperfect information (e.g., behavior in the absence of deposit insurance) are directly relevant. We applied our model to study revenue efficiency and competition in the retail deposit market of the CEE banking industry.

---

[14]We also estimated a simultaneous equation model for revenue efficiency and the Lerner Index. The results are consistent in supporting the U-shape type of relationship between these two variables. An implication of this finding is that there may be support for the 'quiet life' hypothesis at higher segments of market power.

Our empirical analysis is illustrative rather than exhaustive. Hence, it does not purport to serve as a comprehensive study of monopsony power in CEE banking.

Our findings suggest an inverted U-shaped relationship corroborating previous findings in the literature. We also find that riskier banks, such as those with more impaired loans, and banks that rely more on deposits to fund their assets exert less monopsony power for deposits. Bank profitability on the other hand is positively associated with monopsony power. New liquidity regulations under Basel 3 have increased the reliance of banks on more stable sources of funds. These regulations are designed to reduce rollover risk and may have adverse effects on bank funding costs (see Bloor *et al.*, 2011). However, such requirements may also act as a remedy for monopsony in the deposit market by inducing a more elastic supply of deposits to the relevant bank. As funding costs rise with volumes by more in less-liquid long-term funding markets, those rising costs are likely to drive up the rate paid on retail deposits, thereby attenuating the effects of monopsony power. Our findings suggest a negative relation between higher stable funding ratios and higher competition in the deposits market. As this is preliminary evidence, we leave this topic for further scrutiny in future research. Monopsony power in the deposit market can also have an effect on banks' loan pricing. We too leave this topic to future research.

Acknowledgments

We would like to thank the audience at the University of Queensland's Workshop on Productivity on Healthcare and Other Key Sectors of the Economy, as well as the School of Economics for hosting us.

https://doi.org/10.1142/9789811285936_0005

Chapter 5

Estimating Market Power Using Input Distance Functions

Rolf G. Färe*, Maryam Hasannasab[†], Giannis Karagiannis[‡], and Dimitris Margaritis[†]

*Oregon State University, Corvallis, OR, USA
†University of Auckland, Auckland, New Zealand
‡University of Macedonia, Thessaloniki, Macedonia, Greece

1. Introduction

Recent increases in interest rates following a tightening of monetary conditions by central banks to combat rising inflationary pressures have renewed interest in the pass-through of policy rates to retail interest rates. At the centre of this debate is the degree of market power in the market for loans recognizing that lending spreads have widened considerably. For example, mortgage spreads are now well above those present during the early stages of the COVID-19 pandemic and are approaching levels last seen during the 2008 financial crisis. Similarly, small business loans are now approaching double-digit levels in many OECD countries for the first time in decades raising concerns about the future state of the global economy.

This chapter has two main objectives. First, we rely on the duality between the cost function and the input distance function to derive the monopoly version of the Lerner Index using an input distance function approach. In doing so, we endeavour to avoid the use of input prices which are often not very reliable in practice. Second, we use our measure of the Lerner Index to study the relationship between market structure and firm efficiency. This is important to recognize the potential negative relation between firm efficiency and market power that has received much attention in the literature as well as in policy circles. For example, market structure and efficiency considerations have underpinned deregulatory changes to enhance competition in many industries of both industrialized and developing economies (Bertrand and Mullainathan, 2003, 2007; Koetter *et al.*, 2012).

Market power may result in higher costs (rather than higher profits) due to inefficiencies arising from the reduction of competitive pressures, as the management is under less pressure to minimise costs — the so-called "quiet life effect" (Hicks, 1935; Berger and Hannan, 1998). In contrast, higher bank competition can erode market power, decrease profit margins, and result in reduced franchise value, encouraging banks to take on more risk to increase returns (Keeley, 1990; Berger *et al.*, 2009).

By encompassing a complete characterization of technology in the form of a distance function in the quantity space and its value dual, the cost function, our framework readily models heterogeneous bank behavior with respect to forgoing possible rents in exchange for inefficiencies as required by the quiet life hypothesis (see also Koetter *et al.*, 2012).

Following the theory part presented in Section 2, we apply our version of the Lerner Index to measure monopoly power in the market for bank loans in Section 3. Section 4 concludes the chapter.

2. Analytical Framework

The proposed model is based on the duality between the input distance function (D_i) and the cost function (C). The latter is defined as

$$C(w, y) = \min_x \{w'x : D_i(x, y) \geq 1\}, \quad w > 0 \qquad (1)$$

and it is non-decreasing, concave and linear homogenous in input prices, w, non-decreasing and quasi-convex in outputs, y.[1] Using standard duality results (see Färe and Primont, 1995), it can be shown that the cost function

---

[1] Due to the short panel at hand, it is reasonable to assume that there was no technical change during the three-year period covered by the data, and for this reason, a time trend is not included in either the cost or the distance function.

in (1) is dual to the *input distance function*:

$$D_i(x, y) = \min_{w}\{w'x : C(w, y) \geq 1\}, \quad x \in R_+^N \tag{2}$$

The input distance function is assumed to be linear homogenous, non-decreasing and concave in inputs, x, and non-increasing and quasi-convex in y.

The Lagrangian and the first-order conditions for (1) are given respectively by

$$\Lambda(x, \lambda) = w'x + \lambda(1 - D_i(x, y)) \tag{3}$$

and

$$w_i - \lambda\left(\frac{\partial D_i(x, y)}{\partial x_k}\right) = 0 \tag{4a}$$

$$1 - D_i(x, y) = 0 \tag{4b}$$

where λ is the Lagrangian multiplier. Using the first-order conditions and the linear homogeneity of $D_i(x, y)$ in x, it can be shown (see Färe and Primont, 1995, p. 52) that

$$\lambda(w, y) = C(w, y) \tag{5}$$

In addition, by applying the envelope theorem, the following relation can be obtained:

$$\frac{\partial C(w, y)}{\partial y_j} = -\lambda\frac{\partial D_i(x, y)}{\partial y_j} \tag{6}$$

It is well known in the efficiency literature that the unobserved minimum cost is related to actual cost by the extent of cost inefficiency. To see this, we define cost efficiency (CE) as (see Farrell, 1957)

$$\text{CE} = \frac{C(w, y)}{w'x} = \text{TE} * \text{AE} \tag{7}$$

which as the second equality in (7) shows that it may be attributed to either technical (TE) or allocative (AE) inefficiency, or even both. Then if it is assumed that there is no cost inefficiency, minimum cost coincides with actual cost, and the latter is substituted in (5) and (6) to derive estimates of marginal cost.

Substituting (5) into (6), we obtain

$$\frac{\partial C(w, y)}{\partial y_j} = -C(w, y)\frac{\partial D_i(x, y)}{\partial y_j} \qquad (8)$$

From (8),

$$\frac{\partial C(w, y)}{\partial y_j} = -C(w, y)\left[\frac{\partial D_i(x, y)}{\partial y_j}\frac{y_j}{D_i(x, y)}\right]\frac{D_i(x, y)}{y_j}$$

$$= -\frac{C(w, y)}{y_j}D_i(x, y)e_j \qquad (9)$$

where $e_j = \frac{\partial \ln D_i(x, y)}{\partial \ln y_j}$ is (minus) the reciprocal of the scale elasticity with respect to the jth output.

We can now express cost efficiency (7) as

$$\frac{C(w, y)}{wx} = TE_i * AE_i = \left[\frac{1}{D_i(x, y)}\right]AE_i \Rightarrow C(w, y)D_i(x, y)$$

$$= (w'x)AE_i \qquad (10)$$

Using (9) and (10), we can express marginal cost evaluated at the frontier as

$$\frac{\partial C(w, y)}{\partial y_j} = -\frac{w'x}{y_j}CE_i * e_j \qquad (11)$$

The Lerner Index for output j is given by

$$L_j = \frac{p_j - \frac{\partial C(w, y)}{\partial y_j}}{p_j} \qquad (12)$$

where p_j denotes the price of the jth output. Substituting (11) into (12), we have

$$L_j = \frac{p_j + \left(\frac{w'x}{y_j}\right)CE_i * e_j}{p_j} = \frac{\frac{p_j y_j + (w'x)CE_i * e_j}{y_j}}{p_j} = \frac{p_j y_j + (w'x)CE_i * e_j}{p_j y_j}$$

and thus,

$$L_j = 1 + \left(\frac{w'x}{p_j y_j}\right)CE_i * e_j \qquad (13)$$

To estimate the Lerner Index, we need estimates of CE_i and e_j. The latter is obtained from the estimated input distance function. For the former, we need the estimate of CE_i, which is also obtained from the estimated input distance function and from cost efficiency, as shown in Karagiannis *et al.* (2004).

If there is no cost allocative inefficiency, the Lerner Index is simplified as

$$L_j = 1 + \left(\frac{w'x}{p_j y_j}\right) e_j \tag{14}$$

Note that the same relation is obtained in the single output case. We can rewrite (11) as

$$\frac{\partial C(w, y)}{\partial y_j} = AC * AE_i * e_{cy}$$

where AC denotes average cost, $e_{cy} = \frac{\partial \ln C(w, y)}{\partial \ln y} = -e_j = \frac{\partial \ln D_i(x, y)}{\partial \ln y}$, is the reciprocal of the elasticity of scale, and assuming cost efficiency and marginal cost pricing, $L = 0$. If, however, there is cost inefficiency $C(w, y) = (w'x) * CE$, and thus to estimate the Lerner Index, we need some measure of cost efficiency scores. Fortunately, these can be derived directly from the input distance function regardless of the source of cost inefficiency. In the absence of allocative inefficiency, $CE = TE = 1/D_i(x, y)$, and consequently, $C(w, y) = (wx)/D_i(x, y)$.

In the presence of allocative inefficiency, the calculations become more complicated as the cost minimizing input vector should be derived. Karagiannis *et al.* (2004) have developed a procedure for deriving the cost minimizing input vector x^O by using the notion of virtual prices and dual Shephard's lemma, i.e., $w_j^v = C(w^v, y)(\partial D^I(x, y)/\partial x_j)$ (Färe and Grosskopf, 1990), where w^v denotes the vector of virtual input prices and $C(w^v, y)$ the minimum shadow cost at the observed input mix.[2]

By definition, virtual and market prices coincide at the (unobserved) cost minimizing input vector and consequently $C(w, y) = C(w^v, y)$ and $w_j = C(w, y)(\partial D^I(x, y)/\partial x_j)$. The latter consists of a system of equations that can be solved for the cost minimizing input ratios $(x_j/x_1)^O$ as long as the underlying technology is known and the virtual price of

---

[2] Virtual prices are the input prices that make the (observed) technically inefficient input mix allocatively efficient.

one input (say, the first one) coincides with its market price. The number of unknowns in this system is greater than the number of equations. For this reason, each equation is divided by the first equation in the system to eliminate the minimum cost $C(w, y)$ and then the resulting system of $n - 1$ equations is solved for the $n - 1$ cost minimizing input ratios by assuming that the virtual and market prices of the first input coincide. Then, the following relation

$$\frac{C(w, y)}{x_1} = w_1 + w_2 \left(\frac{x_2}{x_1}\right)^O + \cdots + w_m \left(\frac{x_m}{x_1}\right)^O \qquad (15)$$

can be used to compute AE as follows:

$$\text{AE} = \frac{C(w, y)}{w'x} = \frac{C(w, y)/x_1}{w'x/x_1} \qquad (16)$$

given that $x_1 = x_1^O$.

Finally, in the case of both technical and allocative inefficiency, the right-hand side of (16) should be multiplied by $D_i(x, y)$ in order to obtain the allocative efficiency scores. Technical efficiency is measured as TE $= 1/D^I(x, y)$ and $C(w, y) = (w'x) * \text{TE} * \text{AE}$.

3. Empirical Application

We use the same data as in Chapter 5 obtained from Orbis Bank Focus during the period 2013–2016 to estimate the Lerner Index for bank loans for Central and Eastern Europe (CEE) banks.

The input distance function is parameterized in a translog functional form:

$$\ln D_I(x, y) = \alpha_0 + \sum_{n=1}^{N} \alpha_n \ln x_n + \sum_{m=1}^{M} \beta_m \ln y_m + \frac{1}{2} \sum_{n=1}^{N} \sum_{n'=1}^{N} \alpha_{nn'} \ln x_n \ln x_{n'}$$

$$+ \frac{1}{2} \sum_{m=1}^{M} \sum_{m'=1}^{M} \beta_{mm'} \ln y_m \ln y_{m'} + \sum_{n=1}^{N} \sum_{m=1}^{M} \gamma_{nm} \ln x_n \ln y_{m'}$$

$$\alpha_{nn'} = \alpha_{n'n}, n \neq n'; \quad \beta_{mm'} = \beta_{m'm}, m \neq m' \qquad (17)$$

Instead of using stochastic frontier analysis (SFA), we opt for deterministic linear programming estimation of the input distance function that allows us to impose inequality constraints adhering to the feasibility and monotonicity properties of the input distance function:

$$\min \sum_{k=1}^{n} \ln D_I(x, y) \tag{18}$$

s.t.

$$\ln D_I(x, y) \geq 0, \quad k = 1, \ldots, K, \qquad (\text{feasibility})$$

$$\partial_{\ln y_m} \ln D_I(x, y) \leq 0, \ k = 1, \ldots, K, \quad m = 1, \ldots, M, \quad (\text{monotonicity})$$

$$\partial_{\ln x_n} \ln D_I(x, y) \geq 0, \ k = 1, \ldots, K, \quad n = 1, \ldots, N, \quad (\text{monotonicity})$$

$$\sum_{n=1}^{N} \alpha_n = 1, \quad (\text{homogeneity})$$

$$\sum_{n=1}^{N} \gamma_{nm} = 0, \quad m = 1, \ldots, M,$$

$$\sum_{n'=1}^{N} \alpha_{n\acute{n}} = 0, \quad n = 1, \ldots, N,$$

$$\alpha_{nn'} = \alpha_{n'n}, \ n \neq \acute{n}; \ \beta_{mm'} = \beta_{m'm}, \ m \neq m'. \quad (\text{symmetry})$$

Hence,

$$e_m = \left(\beta_m + \frac{1}{2} \left(\sum_{m'=1}^{M} \beta_{mm'} \ln y_{m'} + \beta_{mm} \ln y_m \right) + \sum_{n=1}^{N} \gamma_{nm} \ln \chi_n^k \right) \tag{19}$$

Substituting (19) into (14), we obtain the Lerner Index for the *m*th output (loans).

Figure 1 shows the averages for the Lerner Index across the years. The index is decreasing from 2013 to 2016, indicating an increasing trend in bank pricing power in the market for loans during these years. This finding is not surprising, recognizing the consolidation in the banking markets in the aftermath of the global financial and sovereign crises in Europe.

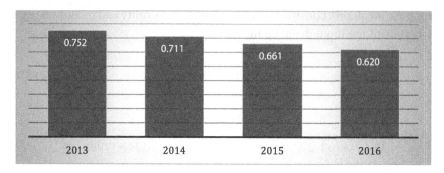

Figure 1.   Lerner Indices for CEE Banks

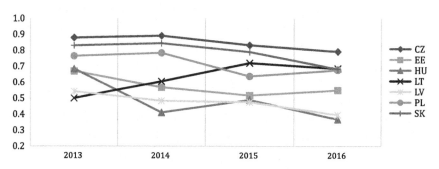

Figure 2.   Lerner Indices across CEE Countries

Figure 2 depicts the Lerner Index averages across different CEE countries for the period 2013–2016.

Figure 3 presents several bank indicators sorted by Lerner Index quartiles. The graphs show that the Lerner Index is decreasing in the cost-to-income ratio (a financial indicator of cost efficiency) and in the loan loss reserves ratio (a measure of asset quality). On the other hand, the Lerner Index is increasing in the interest income to total operating income ratio and in the return on average equity. The evidence presented in these graphs suggests that increasing competitive pressures force banks to improve their cost efficiency, improve asset quality, and improve profitability with more reliance on interest income.

The quantile plots shown in Figure 3 provide *prima facie* evidence in support of the Hicksian "quiet life hypothesis". As aptly put by Hicks (1935), "the best of all monopoly profits is the quiet life", suggesting that

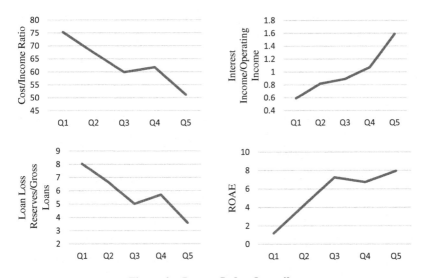

Figure 3. Lerner Index Quantiles

firms with higher market power that are insulated from competition may exhibit lower efficiency as their managers may exert less effort or act in ways that serve their own interests at the expense of shareholders.

The quiet life hypothesis may also be extended to address risk-taking behavior and bank stability. Under the "competition-stability" hypothesis, higher market power in the loan market may be associated with higher bank risk as higher lending rates make it harder for borrowers to repay loans, exacerbating moral hazard and adverse selection problems (Boyd and De Nicolo, 2005; Berger *et al.*, 2009). In contrast, the "competition-fragility" hypothesis predicts that more bank competition can erode market power, decrease profit margins, and result in reduced franchise value, encouraging banks to take on more risk to increase returns (Keeley, 1990; Berger *et al.*, 2009). If anything, the evidence presented in Figure 3 shows that more bank competition is not only associated with lower bank risk (Loan Loss Reserves) but also appears to be associated with higher profits (ROAE).

We turn next to investigate the quiet life hypothesis further by carrying out panel regression estimation. The dependent variable is bank efficiency and the main explanatory variable of interest is the Lerner Index. We present fixed effects estimates with robust standard errors clustered by country for the period, 2013–2016, controlling for bank-specific characteristics

Table 1. Panel Estimation Bank Efficiency

	Coeff.	t-Stat.	Coeff.	t-Stat.	Coeff.	t-Stat.	Coeff.	t-Stat.
Lerner	0.161	2.11	0.159	2.11	0.171	2.25	0.149	4.03
Log TA	0.117	3.11	0.11	2.34	0.117	3.07	0.161	2.89
EQ/TA	0.012	1.68	0.012	1.36	0.012	1.67	0.009	1.87
Cost/Inc			0.0003	0.05	0.0003	0.02		
IntInc/Inc	−0.151	−2.97	−0.156	−3.27	−0.158	−2.99	−0.205	−6.78
RWA/TA	−0.270	−2.47	−0.205	−2.17	−0.28*	−2.67	−0.301	−2.4
NIM	−0.045	−1.73	−0.032	−0.75	−0.043	−1.56	−0.044	−1.82
LLR/LOANS	0.011	1.96			0.01	1.97	0.011	2.22
LQ/STFUND							−0.002	−4.56
Constant	−0.808	−1.23	−0.729	−0.88	−0.833	−1.20	−1.309	−1.38
R^2	0.160		0.131		0.160		0.191	

Notes: Lerner is the Lerner Index for bank loans, Log TA is log of total assets, EQ/TA is equity to total assets, IntInc/Inc is interest income to total operating income, RWA is risk-weighted assets to total assets, NIM is net interest margin, LLR is loan loss reserve, LOANS is gross loans, LQ/STFUND is liquid assets to stable funding (deposits and short-term funding).

(financial indicators). The estimation results are shown in Table 1. The results of Table 1 provide further support for the quiet life hypothesis, demonstrating that an increase in the Lerner Index is associated with greater bank efficiency. We also find that larger as well as better capitalized banks are associated with higher efficiency consistent with a notion of franchise value preservation. On the other hand, we find a negative relation between net interest margins, interest income to total income and liquid assets to stable funding ratios with bank efficiency. The two risk measures have offsetting effects on efficiency, suggesting that more efficient banks tend to carry better-quality assets on their portfolio while exercising more prudency by taking higher reserves for loan losses. This finding is not surprising, when recognizing that the sample period coincides with a stressful period in European banking in the aftermath of the sovereign crisis where many banks engaged in aggressive derisking of their asset portfolios.

4. Conclusion

We have introduced an integrative framework to study bank efficiency and product market structure. Specifically, we used input distance functions to derive a Lerner-type index capturing deviations from competitive behavior in the market for bank loans. We have shown how this index may be estimated using information on input and output quantities, operating cost, and interest income on loans. We applied our method to measure market power in the Central and Eastern European (CEE) market for bank loans. Our findings provide prima facie support for the Hicksian Quiet Life Hypothesis that firms with higher market power that are insulated from competition may exhibit lower efficiency as their managers may exert less effort or act in ways that serve their own interests at the expense of shareholders. Furthermore, we find that larger as well as better capitalized banks are associated with higher efficiency consistent with a notion of franchise value preservation. More efficient banks tend to carry better-quality assets on their portfolio while exercising more prudency by holding higher reserves for loan losses.

https://doi.org/10.1142/9789811285936_0006

Chapter 6

Public and Private Banks in China: Does Public Ownership Confer Monopoly Power?

Bill Weber and Chen Wu

Department of Accounting, Economics and Finance,
Southeast Missouri State University
Cape Girardeau, USA

1. Introduction

In 2018, loans by the banking industry in China accounted for more than 80% of the annual flow of financing to the Chinese real economy (China Statistical Yearbook, 2019). Moreover, Chinese state-owned commercial banks accounted for more than half of total bank assets. To what extent do state-owned banks and other semi-private banks exercise monopoly power in the production of loans to state-owned and private enterprises and in offering securities investments to Chinese savers? In this chapter, we investigate the price efficiency of Chinese banks from 2007 to 2019 using a multi-product Lerner Index. As key financial intermediaries, Chinese state-owned commercial banks (SOCBs) raise deposits from savers to produce a portfolio of interest-bearing assets of loans and securities investments. The Lerner Index measures the extent to which SOCBs charge interest on loans and earn returns on investments greater than the marginal costs of those activities. The lack of well-developed financial markets means market interest rates are usually unknown, with rates more often set by government. In fact, the People's Bank of China sets maximum deposit rates and minimum loan rates, reducing the potential for competition to narrow the spread (Elliott and Kai, 2013). Because SOCBs face little market discipline and investors have poorly defined property rights to bank profits (Yeung, 2021), our approach recovers the shadow prices of the various bank products and compares those prices to marginal costs using the Lerner (1934) index of monopoly power.

The multi-product Lerner Index we develop is preferred to an aggregate Lerner Index for which the conditions necessary for consistent aggregation are overly restricted and have been rejected for US banks (Shaffer and Spierdijk, 2020). Moreover, the Lerner Index is preferred to the often-used Panzar–Rosse (1987) H-statistic of competition which equals the sum of the elasticities of total revenue with respect to the input prices. Shaffer and Spierdijk (2017) showed that the sign of the H-statistic depends on the strategic behavior of firms in the industry such as when firms engage in entry limit pricing or have expense preference behavior.

Färe and Grosskopf (1998) developed shadow pricing formulas for non-marketed outputs and their method has been used to estimate shadow prices for public conservation areas and water pollutants by Färe *et al.* (2001, 2006) and by Fukuyama and Weber (2008) to estimate the charge-off on non-performing loans for Japanese banks. However, the method requires knowledge of at least one market price to obtain the shadow price(s) and market prices might not be observed for public sector producers, such as Chinese banks. This chapter derives output prices for Chinese banks from estimates of an input distance function and the observed costs or budget used by the banks to hire inputs. These prices are compared with marginal costs to construct a multi-product Lerner Index.

Although China has moved toward greater market allocation of financial resources, SOCBs remain the largest source of financial assets and continue to play an important role in allocating scarce capital, especially to state-owned enterprises (Yeung, 2021). If these SOCBs are earning monopoly profits, then inefficiency exists in the financial system which might spillover to the real economy. Section 2 reviews the finance and development nexus and empirical evidence thereon for China. In addition, general background on the structure of China's banking industry and empirical evidence on Chinese bank efficiency is offered. Section 3 derives the pricing formula and constructs the aggregate Lerner Index of monopoly power. Section 4 specifies the translog functions for the input distance function and cost function that are estimated using stochastic frontier analysis. The data and empirical results are in Section 5 and the final section concludes.

2. The Finance/Development Nexus in China

In an early paper, Gurley and Shaw (1955) proposed a link between a country's financial system and its economic development. In general, development is accompanied by the accumulation of debt balanced by financial assets. Direct finance occurs when savers channel their surplus directly to investors, and this type of finance tends to have high transaction costs due to less asset diversification, less liquidity relative to bonds and securities, higher monitoring costs of the lending process, and asymmetric information between savers and borrowers. Thus, in early development, a move toward indirect finance can reduce transaction costs and actively promote growth as banks and other financial institutions channel resources from small savers to large investors. In later stages of development, finance comes to play a more passive role in satisfying the demand for new financial services that arise from a more complex real economy.[1] For more than 40 years, the Chinese economy has grown rapidly with Chinese SOCBs as the dominant financial institutions. The link between finance and development likely depends on the efficiency with which financial institutions transform saving into investment. After years of growth, the Chinese economy has recently slowed. If finance causes growth, various inefficiencies in the banking system might be an underlying cause of the slower growth.

From the 1950s to the 2000s, average annual growth rates in China accelerated from 0.5% to 7.9% but then slowed to 2.9% in the 2010s (see Table 1).[2] Zhu (2012) identifies 1978 as the year when various market and structural reforms began to increase growth in real GDP per capita and total factor productivity. Solow (1959) decomposed economic growth into growth attributable to changes in input usage and a residual measuring total factor productivity growth that arises from gains in

---

[1] See also Patrick (1966).
[2] Author calculations from Penn World Tables 10.0 using geometric means.

Table 1.   Per Capita Real GDP Growth Rates in China

Years	Annual Growth Rate (%)
1952–1960	0.5
1961–1970	4.1
1971–1980	1.9
1981–1990	3.9
1991–2000	5.1
2001–2010	7.9
2011–2019	2.9

efficiency and technical change. Using Solow's method, Zhu (2012) found annual total factor productivity gains of 2.45% during 1988–1998 and 4.68% during 1998–2007. For the state sector, high productivity growth was accompanied by a declining state employment share and a declining state share of GDP.

As financial intermediaries Chinese banks provide loans to state-owned enterprises, private businesses and consumers by offering investment opportunities for savers. These loans and investments affect the allocation of capital to the real economy which affects economic growth and development. Recent research has examined the causal direction(s) between finance and development for the Chinese economy. Chow *et al.* (2018) examined the finance/growth nexus for 30 Chinese cities during 1979–1981 to 2009–2011. Their regime switching model of finance/growth causality tested for bi-directional causality, uni-directional causality or no causality between finance and growth. Using bank loans to proxy financial development and income growth to proxy economic development, the authors found that finance causes growth in Chinese cities located in prosperous regions. In cities located in less developed regions, bi-directional causality and uni-directional causality from finance to growth were observed intermittently.

2.1.   *Background on Chinese banks*

The Chinese financial sector consists of a State Council that is over the central bank called **People's Bank of China**. State-owned commercial banks operate alongside joint-stock commercial banks (JSCBs), city commercial banks (CCBs), rural financial banks (RFBs) and foreign banks (FBs). The China Banking Regulatory Commission oversees most bank activities. State-owned banks controlled approximately 80% of Chinese bank assets during the 1990s and Figure 1 shows that percentage falling during 2007–2019. In the same period, the asset share of JSCBs increased from 20% to 23%, the share of CCBs increased from 4% to 14%, the share of RFBs increased from 1% to 4% and the share of FBs grew from 0% to 1%. In the early post-1978 reform period, many SOEs (state-owned enterprises) were changed into shareholding companies. The former SOEs were given easy access to bank credit relative to lower-level governments and private domestic firms. During 1988–1998, SOCBs continued to bail out SOEs which took away the threat of "exit" as part of the market process that reallocates capital from low-valued uses to high-valued uses and is a source of productivity growth. As a consequence, non-performing loans (NPLs) of SOCBs increased rapidly to the point where those banks would likely have been insolvent in a free market system.

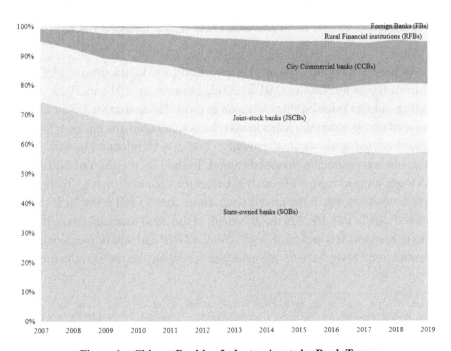

Figure 1. Chinese Banking Industry Assets by Bank Type

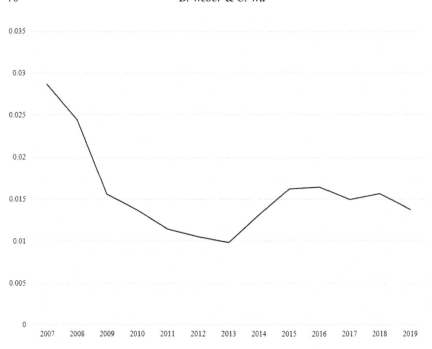

Figure 2. Ratio of Non-Performing Loans to Total Loans for SOCBs

As shown in Figure 2, the proportion of NPLs to total loans for SOCBs fell from 0.029 in 2007 to 0.01 in 2013, but rose to 0.013 in 2019. The bursting of asset price bubbles in Japan in the 1990s and in the US in 2008 increased non-performing loans held by banks. In Japan, the ensuing "lost" decade resulted in slower real growth as banks were reluctant to write-off bad loans and reallocate financial capital. In the US, the ratio of NPLs to total loans jumped from 0.6% in 2006 before the financial crisis to 5% in the immediate aftermath of the crisis. Then, from 2010 to 2017, the NPL ratio declined slowly to 1.1%.[3] In the aftermath of the 2008 financial crisis, bank loans to business fell and as of 2019, US real GDP had still not regained its potential trend level.[4] Given the evidence for Japan and the US, the recent

---

[3]Federal Reserve Bank of St. Louis–Bank Non-Performing Loans to Gross Loans for United States, Percent, Annual, Not Seasonally Adjusted, https://fred.stlouisfed.org/series/DDSI02USA156 NWDB.
[4]Federal Reserve Bank of St. Louis Economic Data: Real potential GDP and actual real GDP: GDPPOT and GDPC1.

Table 2. One Year Loan and Deposit Interest Rates

Year	Loan Rate (%)	Deposit Rate (%)	Spread (%)
2010	5.8	2.5	3.3
2011	6.6	3.5	3.1
2012	6.0	3.0	3.0
2015	4.9	2.0	2.9

Source: Chinese Statistical Yearbook 2019.

slowdown in Chinese growth seen in Table 1 and its rising NPL proportion suggest a continuing link between finance and development.

Rules on bank branching by Chinese JSCBs were relaxed in 2009 which increased competition. However, while JSCBs expanded their market share, Gao *et al.* (2019) found that the expansion was fueled by lending to SOEs. Elliott and Yan (2013) suggested that the move toward market discipline in banking was incomplete as most bank managers might face career disruption if making bad loans to private businesses, but those same managers would seldom be terminated if the loans were instead made to SOEs. In 2013, interest rates on loans were deregulated by the State Council to help instill greater market discipline in Chinese banking and improve performance in the real economy. But, as shown in Table 2, while one year interest rates moved up and down during 2010–2015, interest rate spreads declined by only 0.1% during the deregulated period 2012–2015. Thus, skepticism is in order concerning whether the deregulatory efforts had much effect on the interest spread. Furthermore, Fungacova and Weill (2017) find no increase in competition among Chinese banks using an aggregate Lerner Index during 2004–2014.

2.2. *Chinese bank efficiency studies*

China's capital market is relatively underdeveloped and its financial system is dominated by highly regulated banks that provide liquidity to firms in physical production (Huang *et al.*, 2020). Five large SOCBs hold more than 50% of total bank assets. A consensus exists that SOCBs pursue objectives such as maximizing employment or providing credit to favoured industries, rather than engaging in marginal cost pricing of loans and securities investments. In addition, the state sometimes injects credit into the banking system as a form of fiscal policy (Elliott and Yan, 2013; Yeung, 2021). Huang *et al.* (2017) evaluated banks' efficiency under different ownership forms in a two-stage production model where stage 1 produces deposits which are used in stage 2 to produce a portfolio of loans, investments and non-interest income. Their data used 5 large national commercial banks (LNCBs), 12 joint-stock commercial banks (JSCBs) and 82 city and rural commercial banks from 2002 to 2015. JSCBs were found to be most efficient in both production stages while the LNCBs were least efficient.

Saunders *et al.* (2021) explain how changing consumer preferences, technologies and macroeconomic conditions change the regulatory burden faced by banks. For instance, interest rate ceilings on deposits and floors on loans affect savings and investment flows. As a result, less regulated financial entities — called shadow banks — often step in to fill any void. Like in the US and other countries, various unregulated shadow banking activities have emerged in China. Ding *et al.* (2020) examined three shadow banking activities: the making of entrusted loans which are company-to-company loans which go through a bank, the making of interbank loans designed to circumvent maximum loan restrictions and minimum reserve requirements, and rendering other financial services in the form of investment receivables and off-balance sheet contingencies that generate fee income. The authors estimated bank profit and cost functions assuming three outputs (consumer loans, deposits and other earning assets) and two inputs (deposits and non-interest expenses) for 272 banks during 2002–2016 and found that shadow banks were less efficient than city commercial banks.

In 2010, The Memorandum of Understanding and the Economic Cooperation Framework Agreement allowed Chinese and Taiwanese banks to engage in cross-border banking. Battese *et al.* (2004) measured efficiency and technical change for distinct groups of producers. Their metafrontier is the envelope of the separate frontiers of different producer groups which allows producers to be benchmarked against their own group and against the metafrontier. Chen *et al.* (2020) used a metafrontier to compare profit inefficiency for Taiwanese and Chinese banks during 2010–2014. Their multi-product model included two outputs (loans and investments) and three inputs (financial funds, labor and quasi-fixed capital). Taiwanese banks were less efficient than Chinese banks relative to the metafrontier, but Taiwanese banks had greater productivity catch up to the metafrontier while Chinese banks diverged from the metafrontier.

Jia (2016) reviewed 20 studies that measured Chinese bank efficiency and tested various hypotheses regarding the effects of state ownership. One hypothesis is that SOCBs are more efficient because the state can channel funds toward sectors with high social returns more easily than their private bank counterparts who are likely focused on maximizing private returns. In addition, the managers of SOCBs are not subject to the vagaries of the market and can better pursue long-term objectives than their private bank counterparts. Furthermore, size and structure regulations that limit single foreign investors from acquiring more than 20% of Chinese bank stocks and an overall limit of 25% on foreign capital limit the ability of private banks to realize economies of scale. An alternative hypothesis asserts that SOCBs are less efficient than for-profit banks because their managers are more often interested in political objectives or their own self-interest because they lack a profit motive and incentives to minimize costs. Furthermore, the "quiet life" hypothesis of J.R. Hicks (1935) suggests that the managers of monopoly firms may face sharply increasing subjective costs from the exertion of finding the profit maximizing price and quantity and might instead prefer a quiet life earning lower profits than might be possible. In China, bank managers might also prefer a quiet life rather than face criticisms from the state apparatus from earning too high profits. In general, the studies reviewed by Jia found that joint stock banks were more efficient than state-owned banks. In addition, the quiet life hypothesis was not supported, primarily because interest rates were administered, rather than market determined.

According to a review by Klapper *et al.* (2009), the Chinese banking industry is dominated by SOCBs and remains mostly closed to foreign interests. In 2005, Chinese banks had lower returns on assets, fewer bank branches and a higher proportion of bank assets to GDP than other Asian developing countries. From 1997 to 2005, the share of bank assets controlled by government declined from 100% to 69%, the private share increased from 0 to 29%, and foreign bank ownership increased from 0 to 2%, after various banking sector reforms that began in 2001. China's entry into the WTO in 2001 brought pressure to reform the banking sector. The "Big Four" banks — Agricultural Bank of China, Bank of China, China Construction Bank and the Industrial and Commercial Bank of China — are state-owned banks and their efficiency has been compared to banks with other ownership forms. Banks with majority foreign ownership were most efficient, followed by private domestic banks, non-big four SOCBs and the Big Four (Berger *et al.*, 2009).

In a three-stage DEA model, Fukuyama and Tan (2019) used deposits and market power in deposits as intermediate products that are used to produce loans and market power in loans. Market power in deposits and loans is measured as the share of deposits and share of loans controlled by a specific bank relative to the banking industry. Furthermore, market power in deposits serves to expand the stage 2 technology thereby allowing greater potential intermediate products to emerge from stage 2. For 792 Chinese bank/year observations, mean bank inefficiencies declined from 2007–2017. However, the authors left unaddressed whether banks with higher market power were also more inefficient, as most economic models posit that firms with market power drive output prices upward by reducing output. An additional aspect of their model came from their use of loan loss provisions as an intermediate product of stage 2. Loan loss provisions provide a safety net should actual loan losses occur and allow greater production of final outputs (interest income and non-interest income) in stage 3 by reducing risk and helping alleviate regulatory/investor concerns about whether the bank can avoid adverse events and remain a going concern.

Qin and Shaffer (2014) specify a supply/demand model for Chinese bank loans using data from 1986–2001. Estimates from their two equation model found no significant difference between price and marginal cost. Related to our work, Fukuyama and Tan (2020) used DEA and estimated the dual multiplier form of the cost function for Chinese banks during 2010–2018. The dual cost function allowed recovery of the marginal cost of total bank assets. Given return on assets and marginal cost, the authors calculated the Lerner Index of monopoly power. They found that Chinese banks had significant market power with a Lerner Index that ranged from 0.9 to 0.96. Joint-stock commercial banks and city commercial banks had less market power than state-owned banks, rural commercial banks and foreign banks.

Our theoretical approach and empirical example differs from Fukuyama and Tan in several ways. First, we use a stochastic approach to recover the banking technology as represented by the cost and input distance functions, which allows confidence intervals to be constructed for the Lerner Index and its components at various points of approximation. Second, although the Fukuyama and Tan approach can recover marginal costs when banks produce multiple outputs, their empirical example included only a single bank output (total assets), whereas we study a two-output example. Third, we estimate shadow prices for the bank outputs, rather than use return on assets as the output price.

3. Constructing a Lerner Index

This section recovers the unobserved output prices using production theory results found in Färe *et al.* (2020). The recovered prices are found from the curvature conditions of the input technology set and an observed budget. These prices are used to construct a Lerner Index for each individual output which can then be aggregated to a multi-product Lerner Index. The method allows public sector agents to engage in the typical monopoly practice of pricing above marginal cost or to engage in "predatory pricing" below marginal cost as an entry deterrent. The theory can be used to determine public sector market power when market prices are not observed, like for Chinese banks where resources are allocated by the state rather than a market process. Marginal costs are derived from the output gradient vector of the estimated cost function.

We assume that banks use inputs $x \in R_+^N$ to produce outputs $y \in R_+^M$. Inputs are paid prices $w \in R_+^N$. Actual costs of production are $c = wx$.

The technology is represented by the input requirement set defined as

$$L(y) = \{x : x \text{ can produce } y\} \tag{1}$$

This set gives the feasible input combinations, x, that can produce observed outputs, y. Axioms of the technology are given in Färe and Primont (1995). Given $L(y)$ and input prices, w, the cost function is defined as

$$C(y, w) = \min_x \{wx : x \in L(y)\} \tag{2}$$

The cost function is homogeneous of degree +1 in input prices, i.e., $C(y, \lambda w) = \lambda C(y, w)$, $\lambda > 0$.

Shephard's (1953) input distance function is used to recover the unobserved output prices of each output. The input distance function is defined on the input requirement sets as

$$D_i(y, x) = \max_{\delta} \ \{\delta : (x/\delta) \in L(y)\} \tag{3}$$

i.e., it seeks the largest feasible radial contraction of the observed input vector.[5] This function represents the input requirement set

$$D_i(y, x) \geq 1 \quad \text{if and only if } x \in L(y) \tag{4}$$

and is homogeneous in input quantities, i.e., $D_i(y, \lambda x) = \lambda D_i(y, x)$, $\lambda > 0$, which follows from its definition.

When a single output is produced, the Lerner Index is given by

$$L = \frac{p - dC(y, w)/dy}{p}$$

$$L = \frac{p - MC}{p} \tag{5}$$

where p is the output price and $dC(y, w)/dy = MC$ is the marginal cost. Under perfect competition or marginal cost pricing regulation, we have $p = MC$ and $L = 0$.

In cases where firms produce multiple outputs, we follow Baumol *et al.* (1982) and define separate indexes for each output, i.e.,

$$L_m = \frac{p_m - \partial C(y, w)/\partial y_m}{p_m}, \quad m = 1, \ldots, M \tag{6}$$

Next, we want to identify the unknown (shadow) prices of the outputs. To do so, we use the profit function which can be defined in terms of the input distance function using a duality result found in Färe and Primont (1995). Let $p \in R_+^M$ represent the vector of output prices. Note that if (x, y) is feasible for a given technology, then $x \in L(y)$ and we may write

---

[5]Note for $x \notin L(y)$, it is defined as the smallest radial expansion of x.

the profit function as

$$\pi(w, p) = \max_{x,y} \ py - wx, \quad \text{s.t. } x \in L(y) \tag{7}$$

where py is the revenue, wx is the cost and $py - wx$ is the profit. The solution to (7) seeks maximum profit by choosing outputs, y, and inputs, x, to maximize $py - wx$ subject to the constraint that the inputs can produce the outputs, i.e., $x \in L(y)$. Therefore, we can use the input distance function to represent the input requirement set in the profit function

$$\pi(w, p) = \max_{x,y} \ py - \frac{wx}{D_i(y, x)} \tag{8}$$

i.e., the profit function can be derived by maximizing the difference between revenue py and observed cost wx normalized by the input distance function, $\frac{wx}{D_i(y,x)}$.

The first-order conditions of the profit maximization problem (8) yield prices

$$p_m = -\frac{wx}{D_i(y, x)^2} \partial D_i(y, x)/\partial y_m, \quad m = 1, \dots, M \tag{9}$$

These prices are recovered from estimates of the parameters of an input distance function and observed costs.

Given the prices p_m, $m = 1, \dots, M$, and marginal costs, $\partial C(y, w)/\partial y_m$, $m = 1, \dots, M$, we use the "denominator rule" following Färe and Karagiannis (2017) and derive a multi-product Lerner Index. Let the weights for the Lerner Index for each output be s_m, $m = 1, \dots, M$, with $\sum_{m=1}^{M} s_m = 1$ with weights chosen as the shadow revenue of each output as a proportion of total shadow revenues:

$$s_m = \frac{p_m y_m}{\sum_{m=1}^{M} p_m y_m}, \quad m = 1, \dots, M \tag{10}$$

Then, the aggregate Lerner Index takes the form

$$L = \sum_{m=1}^{M} s_m L_m \tag{11}$$

Our method described above controls for production inefficiency and cost inefficiency and is related to the work of Koetter *et al.* (2012). These researchers estimated Lerner indices for large US commercial banks from stochastic frontier profit and cost functions. Instead of using observed output prices in the Lerner Index, the authors estimated average revenues from a frontier profit function and we revisit their approach in Section 4.2.

4. Stochastic Estimation Method

4.1. *Functional forms*

We approximate the true technology by estimating translog cost and input distance functions. The translog function provides a flexible second-order approximation to the true but unknown function. In addition, the parameters of the translog form can be constrained to satisfy first-order homogeneity for w in the cost function and for x in the input distance function.

Schmidt and Lovell (1979) developed stochastic frontier analysis (SFA) to estimate technical and allocative inefficiencies. We follow their work and Coelli *et al.* (2005) and specify a two-part error term consisting of (i) randomness and (ii) inefficiency, for a translog input distance function and a translog cost function. The estimates can be used to measure input technical efficiency and cost efficiency, although our main goal is to recover the parameter estimates to use in the pricing formula (9) and to estimate marginal cost.

We assume that $k = 1, \ldots, K$ producers are observed in $t = 1, \ldots, T$ periods. We allow for first-order differences in efficiency and prices between SOCBs and other banks by including an indicator variable $\text{SOCB}_k^t = 1$ for SOCBs and $\text{SOCB}_k^t = 0$ for other banks. In addition, we control for the amount of fee income earned by banks via the exogenous variable $z_k^t =$ fee income. The translog input distance function takes the form

$$\ln D_i(y_k^t, x_k^t) = \alpha_0 + \alpha_s \text{SOCB}_k^t + \sum_{m=1}^{M} \alpha_m \ln y_{mk}^t + \sum_{m=1}^{M} \alpha_{sm} \text{SOCB}_k^t \ln y_{mk}^t$$

$$+ \sum_{n=1}^{N} \beta_n \ln x_{nk}^t + \sum \beta_{sn} \text{SOCB}_k^t \ln x_{nk}^t$$

$$+ 0.5 \left(\sum_{m=1}^{M} \sum_{m'=1}^{M} \alpha_{mm'} \ln y_{mk}^t \ln y_{m'k}^t + \sum_{n=1}^{N} \sum_{n'=1}^{N} \beta_{nn'} \ln x_n^t \ln x_{n'}^t \right)$$

$$+ \sum_{m=1}^{M} \sum_{n=1}^{N} \delta_{mn} \ln x_{nk}^t \ln y_{mk}^t + \theta_1 \ln z_k^t + \theta_2 \, \mathrm{SOCB}_k^t \ln z_k^t + 0.5\theta_3 (\ln z_k^t)^2$$

$$+ \sum_{t=2}^{T} \tau_t d_k^t + \epsilon_k^t \tag{12}$$

where $\epsilon_k^t = v_k^t - \mu_k^t$ is the two-part error term where v_k^t has a symmetric distribution with $E(v_k^t) = 0$ and μ_k^t is a non-negative variable associated with technical inefficiency. We allow technical progress/regress by including time indicator variables, d_k^t, for $T - 1$ of the periods. These time indicators allow the frontier technology technology to shift. We drop the $t = 1$ indicator in the estimation process to avoid exact linear dependence between the time indicators. Relative to $t = 1$, technical progress is indicated by $\tau_t > 0$ and technical regress indicated by $\tau_t < 0$. Linear homogeneity of $D_i(y, x)$ in x constrains the parameters of the translog function such that $\sum_{n=1}^{N} \beta_n = 1$, $\sum_{n=1}^{N} \beta_{sn} = 1$, $\sum_{n'=1}^{N} \beta_{nn'} = 0$, $n = 1, \ldots, N$, and $\sum_{n=1}^{N} \delta_{mn} = 0$, $m = 1, \ldots, M$. Symmetry of the second-order effects assumes that $\beta_{nn'} = \beta_{n'n}$ and $\alpha_{mm'} = \alpha_{m'm}$.

Input technical efficiency (TE) equals the reciprocal of the input distance function with $0 \leq \mathrm{TE} \leq 1$. Estimates of technical efficiency are recovered as

$$\hat{\mathrm{TE}}_k^t = \frac{1}{\hat{D}_i(y_k^t, x_k^t)} = \exp(-\hat{\mu}_k^t), \quad k = 1, \ldots, K, \quad t = 1, \ldots, T \tag{13}$$

From the pricing formula (9) we see that all else equal, increases in TE increase the estimated output prices.

The translog cost function takes the form

$$\ln C(y_k^t, w_k^t) = a_0 + a_s \mathrm{SOCB}_k^t + \sum_{m=1}^{M} a_m \ln y_{mk}^t + \sum_{m=1}^{m} a_{sm} \mathrm{SOCB}_k^t \ln y_{mk}^t$$

$$+ \sum_{n=1}^{N} c_n \ln w_{nk}^t + \sum_{n=1}^{N} c_{sn} \mathrm{SOCB}_k^t \ln w_{nk}^t$$

$$+ 0.5 \left(\sum_{m=1}^{M} \sum_{m'=1}^{M} a_{mm'} \ln y_{mk}^t \ln y_{m'k}^t + \sum_{n=1}^{N} \sum_{n'=1}^{N} c_{nn'} \ln w_{nk}^t \ln w_{n'k}^t \right)$$

$$+ \sum_{m=1}^{M} \sum_{n=1}^{N} h_{mn} \ln y_{mk}^{t} \ln w_{nk}^{t} + \theta_1 \ln z_k^t + \theta_2 \text{SOCB}_k^t \ln z_k^t + \theta_3 (\ln z_k^t)^2$$

$$+ \sum_{t=2}^{T} \tau_t d_k^t + \xi_k^t \tag{14}$$

The two-part residual for the cost function is $\xi_k^t = \psi_k^t + \omega_k^t$, where ψ_k^t has a symmetric distribution with $E(\psi_k^t) = 0$ and ω_k^t is a non-negative variable that determines cost inefficiency as $ci_k^t = 1 - \exp(-\omega_k^t)$. We include time indicators for each period in the cost function and drop the $t = 1$ indicator in the estimation process. These time indicators allow the minimum cost frontier to shift in periods $t = 2, \ldots, T$. Relative to period $t = 1$, technical progress occurs when $\tau_t < 0$ and technical regress occurs when $\tau_t > 0$. Linear homogeneity of the cost function constrains the parameters such that $\sum_{n=1}^{N} c_n = 1$, $\sum_{n=1}^{N} c_{sn} = 1$, $\sum_{n'=1}^{N} c_{nn'} = 0$, $n = 1, \ldots, N$, and $\sum_{m=1}^{M} h_{mn} = 0$, $n = 1, \ldots, N$ and symmetry of the second-order effects means $a_{mm'} = a_{m'm}$ and $c_{nn'} = c_{n'n}$.

Marginal cost for the translog function is calculated as

$$\text{MC}_m = \frac{\partial C}{\partial y_m} = \frac{\partial \ln C}{\partial \ln y_m} \frac{C}{y_m}$$

$$= \left(\frac{a_m + a_{sm} \text{SOCB}_k^t + \sum_{m'=1}^{M} a_{mm'} \ln y_{m'k}^t + \sum_{n=1}^{N} h_{mn} \ln w_{nk}^t}{y_{mk}^t} \right) C_k^t,$$

$$m = 1, \ldots, M \tag{15}$$

Using the pricing formula (9), the shadow prices for the translog model are estimated as[6]

$$p_m = -\frac{w_k^t x_k^t}{D_i(y_k^t, x_k^t)^2} \frac{\partial D_i(y, x)}{\partial y_m}$$

$$= -\frac{wx}{D_i(y_k^t, x_k^t)} \left(\frac{a_m + a_{sm} SOCB_k^t + \sum_{m'=1}^{M} a_{mm'} \ln y_{mk}^t + \sum_{n=1}^{N} \delta_{mn} \ln x_{nk}^t}{y_{mk}^t} \right),$$

$$m = 1, \ldots, M \tag{16}$$

---

[6]Note that $\frac{\partial D_i(y,x)}{\partial y_m} = \frac{\partial \ln D_i(y,x)}{\partial \ln y_m} \frac{D_i(y,x)}{y_m}$.

4.2. Related work

In a dynamic competition model, Kutlu and Sickles (2012) account for inefficiency when estimating marginal cost. Their rationale is that each firm uses its perceived stochastic cost function, $C_k = \tilde{C}_k \exp(u_k)$, to calculate its marginal cost. Therefore, the cost inefficiency, ci_k^t, determined by competing firms affects marginal cost. In this case, marginal cost takes the form

$$
\begin{aligned}
\mathrm{MC}_m &= \frac{\partial \tilde{C}}{\partial y_m} = \frac{\partial \ln \tilde{C}}{\partial y_m} \frac{\tilde{C}}{1 - ci} \\
&= \left(\frac{a_m + a_{sm} \mathrm{SOCB}_k^t + \sum_{m'=1}^{M} a_{mm'} \ln y_{m'k}^t + \sum_{n=1}^{N} h_{mn} \ln w_{nk}^t}{y_{mk}^t} \right) \left(\frac{C}{1 - ci_k^t} \right),
\end{aligned}
$$
$$
m = 1, \ldots, M \tag{17}
$$

When a firm is cost efficient, $ci_k^t = 0$ and marginal cost is given by (15). Cost inefficiency increases the firm's marginal cost which causes it to reduce output further than a monopolist would and results in a larger deadweight loss relative to a cost efficient producer.

Koetter *et al.* (2012) estimated a Lerner Index for US banks. Their method estimated translog profit and cost functions and allowed multiple outputs but defined average revenue on a single aggregate output (Y) as price (P) in the Lerner Index. Average revenue, AR, is

$$
\mathrm{AR} = \frac{\pi(w, p) - C(y, w)}{Y} = \frac{\mathrm{TR}}{Y} \tag{18}
$$

where total revenue, $\mathrm{TR} = py$, is found by substituting $py - wx$ for $\pi(w, p)$ and wx for $C(y, w)$. To complete the index, the authors assumed that the marginal cost of the aggregate output, Y, equals the sum of the individual output marginal costs, i.e., $\mathrm{MC} = \sum_{m=1}^{M} \frac{\partial \ln C}{\partial \ln y_m} \frac{C}{y_m}$. Aggregate bank output equals the sum of the individual bank outputs of total loans and total securities. When banks are not fully efficient, the Lerner Index is biased downward since greater efficiency would result in higher average revenue at lower marginal cost. The authors found that during 1976–2007, a period in which there was substantial geographical deregulation (unit banking and interstate banking restrictions were relaxed), US banks experienced increased market power. However, subsequent research by Shaffer and Spierdijk (2020) showed that the conditions necessary for aggregating multiple outputs to a single bank output are restrictive and were rejected for US banks.

A third related work is by Fukuyama and Tan (2020), referred to earlier. They estimated a Lerner Index for a single bank output using the dual form of the DEA cost function:

$$C(y, w) = \max_{v,\mu,\omega} \{\mu y + \omega:$$

$$-\sum_n v_n x_{nk} + \mu y_k + \omega \leq 0, \quad k = 1, \ldots, k,$$

$$v_n \leq w_n, \quad n = 1, \ldots, N, \quad \mu \geq 0, \quad \omega \text{ free}\} \quad (19)$$

From this dual DEA cost function, the marginal cost of the single output is MC $= \partial C(y, w)/\partial y = \mu^*$, where μ^* is part of the solution to (19). Fukuyama and Tan (2020) used total bank assets as the output and the return on assets as the price of that output. Their estimates of the Lerner Index for 38 Chinese banks from 2010–2018 ranged from 0.96 to 0.93.

5. Data and Estimates

5.1. *Data*

We use an unbalanced panel of 663 Chinese banks that produced during 2007–2019.[7] The sample consists of 60 bank/year observations on state-owned commercial banks (SOCBs) and 603 observations on other banks which include joint-stock commercial banks (JSCBs), city commercial banks (CCBs) and foreign banks (FBs). Table 3 reports the numbers of

---

[7]We deleted banks for which there was incomplete information on inputs, outputs or input prices in a given year.

Table 3. Number and Type of Banks in the Sample

Years	SOCBs	JSCBs	CCBs	FBs
2007	3	7	13	1
2008	4	6	17	1
2009	4	8	24	1
2010	4	8	27	2
2011	4	7	35	2
2012	5	9	44	2
2013	5	9	37	2
2014	5	9	36	4
2015	6	9	42	4
2016	5	9	44	5
2017	5	9	46	5
2018	5	9	48	4
2019	5	8	47	3
Totals	60	107	460	36

sample banks by type in each year. The data were obtained from the China Stock Market and Accounting Research Database (CSMAR).

We follow other bank efficiency researchers and assume that banks use labor (x_1), quasi-fixed capital (x_2) and deposits (x_3) to produce net loans (y_1) and securities investments (y_2). Net loans equal total loans minus non-performing loans. Various research has modeled non-performing loans as an undesirable byproduct of the normal lending process. Furthermore, a variety of research has included deposits as an input, deposits as an output or deposits as an intermediate product. We opt for a more parsimonious model and include net loans as an output and deposits as an input. In addition, we control for the amount of fee income (z) that banks generate from offering other financial services. Including fee income allows exogenous shifts in the frontier technology represented by the distance function and cost function. Thus, banks with the same outputs/inputs might have different levels of technical/cost efficiency dependent on the fee income they earn. The money values for costs, net loans, investments, quasi-fixed capital and deposits have been

Table 4.   Descriptive Statistics

| | | SOCBs | | Other Banks | |
Description	Variable	Mean	Std. Dev.	Mean	Std. Dev.
Net loans	y_1	7402117	3444158	366834	688607
Investments	y_2	3073526	1733251	225209	426300
Labor	x_1	7054	2990	343	609
Fixed capital	x_2	127840	53845	3650	7170
Deposits	x_3	10592593	4579028	478545	811053
Price of x_1	w_1	10.16	1.01	10.16	1.09
Price of x_2	w_2	0.10	0.02	0.14	0.27
Price of x_3	w_3	0.02	0.01	0.03	0.01
Fee income	z	79581	40886	4687	11577
Costs	wx	304911	117330	20921	37293
Size	Assets	14112765	6013217	768655	1365734

deflated by the Chinese GDP deflator and are in millions of Chinese yuan.

Banks report payroll costs but not wages per employee. Instead, we use the average real Chinese wage rate as the price of labor, w_1.[8] The number of employees at each bank, x_1, equals payroll divided by the wage rate. Quasi-fixed capital equals the real value of fixed assets and its price, w_2, equals the ratio of depreciation to fixed assets. The price of deposits, w_3, equals the ratio of interest expense to total deposits.

Table 4 reports descriptive statistics. Average assets of SOCBs are more than 18 times greater than the average assets of other banks. Similarly, SOCBs produce net loans and investments that are 20 and 14 times greater than other banks. Average labor, fixed capital and deposits at SOCBs are 20, 35 and 22 times more than the averages at other banks. Fee income at SOCBs is 17 times greater than that of other banks. All banks face the same wage rate each year, but wages vary by year. Wage rates are deflated by the GDP deflator and average 10.16e5 Chinese yuan. SOCBs pay lower prices

[8]Wage data were taken from the Statistical Yearbook of China 2019 which reports the average wage of employed persons in urban non-private units by year, http://www.stats.gov.cn/tjsj/ndsj/2021/indexeh.htm.

for fixed capital, 10% vs. 14%, and pay less for deposits 2% vs. 3%, than the prices paid by other banks.

5.2. *Estimates*

We impose homogeneity of the translog input distance function by choosing $\lambda = \frac{1}{x_1}$. Thus, $D_i(y, \frac{x}{x_1}) = \frac{1}{x_1}D_i(y, x)$ which means $\ln D_i(y, \frac{x}{x_1}) = -\ln x_1 + \ln D_i(y, x)$. Rearranging yields $-\ln x_1 = \ln D_i(y, \frac{x}{x_1}) - \ln D_i(y, x)$, where $\ln D_i(y, \frac{x}{x_1})$ takes the translog form and $\ln D_i(y, x) = \mu$ in (12). The stochastic estimates are reported in Table 5 and these coefficient estimates are used in the pricing formula (16). All estimates are from the statistical package STATA.

To avoid an exact linear dependence among the indicator variables, we drop the $t = 2007$ indicator (d_{2007}) from the estimation process. A positive indicator coefficient indicates technical progress as the observation (y_k^t, x_k^t) is further from the frontier isoquant in a particular period relative to the 2007 frontier, i.e., the frontier of $L(y)$ shifted inward toward the origin. Likewise, a negative coefficient means the bank is closer to the frontier in the particular year relative to 2007. Positive time coefficients occur for 2008–2010 and for 2014–2019 and negative coefficients occur for 2011–2013. Although the 2018 coefficient is the only coefficient statistically different from zero, we test and reject the null hypothesis that the time coefficients are jointly equal to zero ($\chi^2_{12} = 51.6, p < 0.01$).

For the pooled samples, technical efficiency calculated from (13) averages 0.90 for both SOCBs and other banks. Over 2007–2019, the range of average TE is 0.87 in 2018 to 0.92 in 2011 for SOCBs. For other banks, average TE is 0.90 in every year except 2014, when its average is 0.92.

We impose homogeneity on the cost function by normalizing costs and input prices by the price of labor, w_1. The translog cost function estimates are reported in Table 6. For the cost function, negative time coefficients indicate technical progress, i.e., lower costs independent of outputs and input prices, while positive time coefficients indicate technical regress. The time coefficients are negative for 2009–2011 and for 2013–2019, and positive in the other periods. We test and reject the null hypothesis that the time coefficients are jointly equal to zero ($\chi^2_{12} = 136, p < 0.01$).

B. Weber & C. Wu

Table 5. Translog Input Distance Function Estimates

Variable	Parameter Estimate	Standard Error	z-Value
Intercept	0.0647	2.043	0.03
SOCB indicator	0.0883	1.487	0.06
$\ln y_1$	−0.4348	0.192	−2.27
$\ln y_2$	−0.3770	0.140	−2.70
$\ln y_1 \times$ SOB	−0.0684	0.181	−0.38
$\ln y_2 \times$ SOB	−0.0079	0.047	−0.17
$\ln y_1^2$	−0.1249	0.016	−8.04
$\ln y_2^2$	−0.0690	0.008	−8.71
$\ln y_1 \ln y_2$	0.0823	0.010	8.09
$\ln x_2$	−0.5007	0.174	−2.88
$\ln x_3$	0.8175	0.531	1.54
$\ln x_2 \times$ SOCB	0.1435	0.077	1.86
$\ln x_3 \times$ SOCB	0.0118	0.154	0.08
$\ln x_2^2$	0.0012	0.012	0.10
$\ln x_3^2$	−0.0645	0.076	−0.85
$\ln x_2 \ln x_3$	0.0656	0.026	2.56
$\ln y_1 \ln x_2$	0.0189	0.013	1.45
$\ln y_1 \ln x_3$	0.0228	0.025	0.91
$\ln y_2 \ln x_2$	−0.0157	0.009	−1.70
$\ln y_2 \ln x_3$	0.0070	0.018	0.38
$\ln z$	−0.0666	0.027	−2.50
$\ln z \times$ SOCB	0.0382	0.159	0.24
$\ln z^2$	0.0107	0.005	2.18
d_{2008}	0.0145	0.044	0.33
d_{2009}	0.0110	0.042	0.26
d_{2010}	0.0198	0.042	0.47
d_{2011}	−0.0434	0.041	−1.06
d_{2012}	−0.0397	0.040	−1.00
d_{2013}	−0.0241	0.041	−0.58
d_{2014}	0.0068	0.042	0.16
d_{2015}	0.0111	0.042	0.26
d_{2016}	0.0657	0.043	1.53
d_{2017}	0.0803	0.043	1.89
d_{2018}	0.1051	0.041	2.57
d_{2019}	0.0425	0.041	1.03
σ_v	0.1259	0.007	
σ_u	0.1408	0.016	

Table 6. Translog Cost Function Estimates

Variable	Parameter Estimate	Standard Error	z-Value
Intercept	2.1333	1.522	1.40
SOCB indicator	2.6233	1.486	1.77
$\ln y_1$	0.1080	0.159	0.68
$\ln y_2$	0.4914	0.116	4.24
$\ln y_1 \times$ SOCB	-0.4220	0.208	-2.03
$\ln y_2 \times$ SOCB	0.0246	0.044	0.56
$\ln y_1^2$	0.1449	0.015	9.76
$\ln y_2^2$	0.0826	0.008	10.73
$\ln y_1 \ln y_2$	-0.0978	0.010	-9.93
$\ln w_2$	-0.2840	0.196	-1.45
$\ln w_3$	1.1995	0.372	3.22
$\ln w_2 \times$ SOCB	0.0772	0.074	1.04
$\ln w_3 \times$ SOCB	-0.2704	0.127	-2.12
$\ln w_2^2$	-0.0020	0.019	-0.10
$\ln w_3^2$	0.1150	0.054	2.13
$\ln w_2 \ln w_3$	-0.0169	0.034	-0.50
$\ln y_1 \ln w_2$	0.0313	0.015	2.12
$\ln y_1 \ln w_3$	-0.0267	0.022	-1.21
$\ln y_2 \ln w_2$	-0.0165	0.012	-1.34
$\ln y_2 \ln w_3$	0.0244	0.017	1.40
$\ln z$	0.0629	0.024	2.66
$\ln z \times$ SOCB	0.2118	0.162	1.31
$\ln z^2$	-0.0080	0.004	-1.81
d_{2008}	0.0307	0.042	0.74
d_{2009}	-0.1368	0.041	-3.35
d_{2010}	-0.1809	0.041	-4.39
d_{2011}	-0.0352	0.039	-0.90
d_{2012}	0.0031	0.037	0.08
d_{2013}	-0.0525	0.039	-1.36
d_{2014}	-0.0789	0.039	-2.02
d_{2015}	-0.1349	0.039	-3.42
d_{2016}	-0.2219	0.041	-5.46
d_{2017}	-0.2005	0.040	-5.01
d_{2018}	-0.1975	0.039	-5.12
d_{2019}	-0.1226	0.039	-3.15
σ_ψ	0.1445	0.004	
σ_ω	0.0008	0.080	

Table 7. Prices, Marginal Costs, Revenue Shares, and
Lerner Indexes

Variable	SOCBs		Other Banks	
	Mean	Std. Dev.	Mean	Std. Dev.
p_1	0.040	0.005	0.043	0.014
p_2	0.016	0.006	0.002	0.148
MC_1	0.023	0.004	0.045	0.016
MC_2	0.010	0.008	0.001	0.209
$s_1 = \frac{p_1 y_1}{p_1 y_1 + p_2 y_2}$	0.862	0.044	0.809	0.083
$s_2 = \frac{p_2 y_2}{p_1 y_1 + p_2 y_2}$	0.138	0.044	0.191	0.083
$L_1 = \frac{p_1 - MC_1}{p_1}$	0.423	0.053	-0.050	0.083
$L_2 = \frac{p_2 - MC_2}{p_2}$	0.298	0.545	-0.391	0.935
$L = s_1 L_1 + s_2 L_2$	0.383	0.023	-0.106	0.077

Table 7 reports the average shadow output prices, marginal costs, shadow revenue shares and the Lerner Indexes for the 60 SOCBs and the 603 other banks. The net loan price (p_1) averages 4% for SOCBs and 4.3% for other banks, with marginal costs of 2.3% for SOCBs and and 4.5% for other banks. The price (return) of investments (p_2) is 1.6% for SOCBs but only 0.2% for other banks. The marginal cost of investments is 1% for SOCBs and 0.1% for other banks. The average share of loans (investments) in bank revenues is 0.86 (0.14) for SOCBs and 0.81 (0.19) for other banks. The SOCBs have an average Lerner Index in loans of 0.42 and 0.30 in investments. The aggregate Lerner Index is the weighted average of the two individual Lerner Indexes using the revenue shares for the two outputs as weights. This index averages 0.38 for SOCBs. In contrast, the other banks have a negative average Lerner Index in both loans (−0.05) and investments (−0.39) and an average aggregate Lerner Index of −0.11.

We estimate prices and marginal costs for SOCBs and other banks at various points of approximation and obtain standard errors of the estimates using the delta method in STATA. First, we use the the mean outputs, inputs and input prices for SOCBs and other banks reported in Table 4 in the marginal cost and pricing formulas (15) and (16). These estimates are reported in the first line of Table 8. Using the mean outputs/inputs, the price estimate for loans is 4.4% for SOCBs and 4% for other banks with marginal costs of loans equal to 2.3% for SOCBs and 4.2% for other banks. For investments, SOCBs earn a shadow price (return) of 1.1% but have a marginal cost of making those investments in 1.9%. Other banks earn a shadow price of 1.3% on investments with a marginal cost of 2.1%. Second, we estimate prices and marginal costs using the yearly mean outputs, inputs and input prices for the SOCBs and other banks and these estimates are also reported in Table 8. Loan prices range from 2.9% to 5.3% for SOCBs and range from 2.6% to 5% for other banks. Prices on securities investments range from 0.6% to 1.2% for SOCBs and from 0.9% to 1.9% for other banks. The marginal cost of making securities investments ranges from 1% to 2.1% for SOCBs and from 1.5% to 3.5% for other banks.

These price and marginal cost estimates indicate that SOCBs under-produce loans and overproduce investments. Several reasons might explain the overproduction of investments. First, securities investments might be a residual asset for banks when there is a dearth of profitable loan opportunities. If these securities investments offer enough liquidity, banks can reallocate their portfolio when profitable loan opportunities become available. Second, Chinese banks might allocate some money to marginally unprofitable securities investments if those investments are low risk and help banks meet risk-based capital requirements. The other banks in the sample have marginal costs for both loans and investments that are greater than their shadow prices. In the following section, we test whether the Lerner Indexes for SOCBs and other banks are statistically different from zero.

5.3. *Does public ownership confer monopoly power?*

The Lerner Indexes are constructed from the estimates of two equations: the translog input distance function and the translog cost function. To obtain standard errors of the Lerner Indexes and test whether monopoly power exists, we estimate each Lerner Index twice. First, given the marginal cost estimates reported in Table 8, we calculate the Lerner Indexes and

B. Weber & C. Wu

Table 8. Prices and Marginal Costs Evaluated at mean Outputs/Inputs/Input Prices by Year (Standard Errors)

Year	SOCBs				Other Banks			
	p_1	p_2	MC_1	MC_2	p_1	p_2	MC_1	MC_2
All	0.044	0.011	0.023	0.019	0.040	0.013	0.042	0.021
	(0.015)	(0.004)	(0.010)	(0.010)	(0.001)	(0.001)	(0.006)	(0.007)
2007	0.029	0.006	0.015	0.010	0.031	0.011	0.032	0.018
	(0.005)	(0.002)	(0.007)	(0.004)	(0.001)	(0.002)	(0.004)	(0.006)
2008	0.053	0.012	0.025	0.019	0.041	0.015	0.043	0.025
	(0.019)	(0.003)	(0.013)	(0.008)	(0.002)	(0.003)	(0.006)	(0.009)
2009	0.038	0.009	0.019	0.014	0.026	0.010	0.027	0.016
	(0.008)	(0.003)	(0.009)	(0.006)	(0.002)	(0.002)	(0.004)	(0.006)
2010	0.038	0.009	0.019	0.015	0.027	0.009	0.028	0.016
	(0.008)	(0.003)	(0.009)	(0.007)	(0.001)	(0.002)	(0.004)	(0.006)
2011	0.045	0.011	0.023	0.018	0.037	0.013	0.040	0.024
	(0.007)	(0.004)	(0.012)	(0.009)	(0.002)	(0.003)	(0.006)	(0.009)
2012	0.051	0.012	0.026	0.021	0.043	0.014	0.047	0.025
	(0.009)	(0.004)	(0.012)	(0.010)	(0.002)	(0.003)	(0.007)	(0.009)
2013	0.047	0.011	0.024	0.019	0.043	0.013	0.047	0.023
	(0.008)	(0.004)	(0.011)	(0.010)	(0.002)	(0.002)	(0.007)	(0.008)
2014	0.049	0.012	0.026	0.021	0.050	0.014	0.051	0.023
	(0.008)	(0.005)	(0.011)	(0.011)	(0.003)	(0.002)	(0.008)	(0.011)
2015	0.046	0.011	0.023	0.017	0.049	0.012	0.050	0.019
	(0.008)	(0.004)	(0.011)	(0.008)	(0.003)	(0.002)	(0.008)	(0.006)
2016	0.039	0.009	0.020	0.015	0.039	0.010	0.040	0.015
	(0.007)	(0.003)	(0.009)	(0.007)	(0.003)	(0.002)	(0.006)	(0.005)
2017	0.041	0.010	0.021	0.016	0.044	0.012	0.044	0.018
	(0.007)	(0.004)	(0.010)	(0.008)	(0.003)	(0.002)	(0.004)	(0.006)
2018	0.04	0.007	0.019	0.011	0.045	0.016	0.044	0.025
	(0.007)	(0.002)	(0.01)	(0.004)	(0.003)	(0.003)	0.006)	(0.010)
2019	0.037	0.007	0.018	0.011	0.045	0.019	0.046	0.035
	(0.007)	(0.002)	(0.009)	(0.004)	(0.003)	(0.007)	(0.006)	(0.021)

standard errors using the delta method. This calculation accounts for the variance in the price estimates. For instance, for loans, SOCBs have $MC_1 = 0.023$ using their mean outputs, input prices and fees. Given this marginal cost, we calculate the Lerner Index for loans and its standard error. We calculate the Lerner Index for securities investments in the same way using $MC_2 = 0.019$. Using the mean outputs/inputs, the loan share is $s_1 = 0.91$ and the securities investment share is $s_2 = 0.09$. These shares

Table 9. Lerner Indexes Evaluated at Mean Outputs/Inputs/Input Prices Given Average Marginal Costs (Standard Errors)

Year	SOCBs			Other Banks		
	L_1	L_2	L_{agg}	L_1	L_2	L_{agg}
All	0.471*	−0.734	0.363*	−0.042	−0.633*	−0.136*
	(0.089)	(0.670)	(0.119)	(0.030)	(0.143)	(0.030)
2007	0.480*	−0.656	0.321*	−0.046	−0.653*	−0.130*
	(0.093)	(0.468)	(0.120)	(0.029)	(0.142)	(0.026)
2008	0.532*	−0.582	0.387*	−0.046	−0.647*	−0.123*
	(0.084)	(0.459)	(0.110)	(0.027)	(0.138)	(0.023)
2009	0.501*	−0.570	0.373*	−0.031	−0.622*	−0.100*
	(0.087)	(0.498)	(0.114)	(0.027)	(0.143)	(0.024)
2010	0.500*	−0.649	0.373*	−0.048	−0.686*	−0.116*
	(0.087)	(0.544)	(0.115)	(0.028)	(0.145)	(0.025)
2011	0.492*	−0.641	0.367*	−0.087*	−0.794*	−0.161*
	(0.087)	(0.575)	(0.118)	(0.029)	(0.154)	(0.025)
2012	0.487*	−0.716	0.367*	−0.082*	−0.755*	−0.145*
	(0.087)	(0.624)	(0.118)	(0.029)	(0.146)	(0.025)
2013	0.484*	−0.684	0.367*	−0.051	−0.706*	−0.113*
	(0.087)	(0.623)	(0.118)	(0.030)	(0.146)	(0.026)
2014	0.474*	−0.725	0.354*	−0.029	−0.621*	−0.086*
	(0.089)	(0.654)	(0.122)	(0.030)	(0.137)	(0.025)
2015	0.497*	−0.587	0.378*	−0.025	−0.524*	−0.078*
	(0.087)	(0.529)	(0.114)	(0.031)	(0.123)	(0.025)
2016	0.494*	−0.614	0.372*	−0.015	−0.469*	−0.064*
	(0.086)	(0.562)	(0.116)	(0.033)	(0.124)	(0.026)
2017	0.488*	−0.683	0.371*	−0.005	−0.506*	−0.055*
	(0.087)	(0.589)	(0.115)	(0.032)	(0.129)	(0.026)
2018	0.520*	−0.519	0.375*	0.026	−0.560*	−0.056*
	(0.086)	(0.411)	(0.109)	(0.030)	(0.164)	(0.030)
2019	0.514*	−0.595	0.359*	−0.018	−0.852*	−0.135*
	(0.087)	(0.439)	(0.113)	(0.033)	(0.354)	(0.046)

Note: *Estimate is significant at 95% confidence level.

are used to estimate the aggregate Lerner Index and its standard error and are reported in Table 9. The Lerner Index estimate for loans is $L_1 = 0.47$ with a 95% confidence interval between 0.29 and 0.65. Although SOCBs have a negative Lerner Index for investments of $L_2 = -0.73$, the 95% confidence interval includes 0. The aggregate Lerner Index for SOCBs is significantly positive at 0.36 with a 95% confidence interval between 0.13 and 0.60. Over 2007–2019, L_1 ranges from 0.47 in 2014 to 0.53 in 2018.

B. Weber & C. Wu

Second, given the price estimates reported in Table 8 we again calculate the Lerner Indexes and their standard errors accounting for the variance in marginal costs. For instance, SOCBs have an estimated price of loans of $p_1 = 0.044$ and estimated price of investments of $p_2 = 0.011$. Given these prices, we report the estimates of the two Lerner output indexes, the aggregate Lerner Index and their standard errors in Table 10.

Table 10. Lerner Indexes Evaluated at mean Outputs and Inputs given Average Prices

Year	SOCBs			Other Banks		
	L_1	L_2	L_{agg}	L_1	L_2	L_{agg}
All	0.484*	−0.683	0.379	−0.041	−0.585	−0.128
	(0.228)	(0.890)	(0.204)	(0.151)	(0.565)	(0.074)
2007	0.466*	−0.654	0.326	−0.026	−0.466	−0.097
	(0.231)	(0.629)	(0.226)	(0.136)	(0.494)	(0.066)
2008	0.516*	−0.572	0.381	−0.038	−0.692	−0.143*
	(0.213)	(0.644)	(0.211)	(0.147)	(0.590)	(0.070)
2009	0.487*	−0.562	0.372	−0.058	−0.612	−0.135
	(0.207)	(0.697)	(0.208)	(0.139)	(0.598)	(0.069)
2010	0.486*	−0.616	0.374	−0.053	−0.743	−0.157*
	(0.204)	(0.746)	(0.208)	(0.142)	(0.626)	(0.069)
2011	0.485*	−0.650	0.366	−0.085	−0.823	−0.196*
	(0.203)	(0.789)	(0.208)	(0.151)	(0.667)	(0.073)
2012	0.485*	−0.731	0.368	−0.102	−0.782	−0.211*
	(0.201)	(0.860)	(0.207)	(0.161)	(0.618)	(0.078)
2013	0.484*	−0.729	0.368	−0.096	−0.735	−0.205*
	(0.198)	(0.877)	(0.205)	(0.162)	(0.590)	(0.078)
2014	0.474*	−0.721	0.357	−0.022	−0.627	−0.131
	(0.200)	(0.902)	(0.208)	(0.156)	(0.548)	(0.074)
2015	0.488*	−0.589	0.374	−0.022	−0.616	−0.141
	(0.202)	(0.760)	(0.207)	(0.162)	(0.498)	(0.075)
2016	0.472*	−0.681	0.348	−0.016	−0.537	−0.120
	(0.203)	(0.832)	(0.209)	(0.157)	(0.486)	(0.073)
2017	0.480*	−0.554	0.380	0.009	−0.464	−0.081
	(0.200)	(0.769)	(0.208)	(0.152)	(0.499)	(0.072)
2018	0.519*	−0.576	0.368	0.023	−0.555	−0.058
	(0.206)	(0.629)	(0.204)	(0.139)	(0.645)	(0.069)
2019	0.501*	−0.510	0.366	−0.026	−0.859	−0.101
	(0.210)	(0.617)	(0.207)	(0.134)	(1.136)	(0.070)

Note: *Estimate is significant at 95% confidence level.

The Lerner Index estimates reported in Tables 9 and 10 are similar, but the Lerner estimates in Table 10 have higher standard errors than the Lerner estimates given in Table 9. Both sets of estimates indicate that SOCBs have monopoly power in loans but not in securities investments.

For the other banks in the sample, the confidence interval for the Lerner Index for loans (L_1) includes 0 indicating marginal cost pricing, which is consistent with these other banks operating in a competitive loan market. For securities investments, the results are less clear for other banks. In Table 9 which accounts for price variation with marginal cost held constant, the estimate is $L_2 = -0.63$ with a 95% confidence interval range from -0.92 to -0.34. In Table 10, accounting for variation in marginal cost holding price constant, the Lerner confidence interval for securities investments includes 0 which would indicate marginal cost pricing.

Table 11 reports the estimates of the Lerner Indexes for the Big Four SOCBs and the smaller state-owned China Bank of Communications. Sun (2020) reports that in 2019, the Big Four SOCBs were the top four banks in the world in terms of assets, tier-one capital

Table 11. Lerner Indexes for Chinese State-owned Banks (Standard Errors)

Name	Mean L_1	L_2	L_{agg}	Assets
Industrial and Commercial Bank	0.436 (0.095)	−0.808 (0.661)	0.324 (0.123)	18598875
People's Construction Bank	0.424 (0.095)	−0.910 (0.818)	0.304 (0.134)	16396087
Agricultural Bank of China	0.426 (0.096)	−0.921 (0.730)	0.304 (0.129)	15587711
Bank of China	0.419 (0.096)	−0.911 (0.859)	0.299 (0.138)	14932679
China Bank of Communications	0.498 (0.089)	−0.439 (0.488)	0.413 (0.106)	6062795

and pretax profits. We use the mean outputs/inputs (calculated over time) for each SOCB and calculate its Lerner Index. Each SOCB has significant monopoly power in loans but not in investments. Among these five SOCBs, China Bank of Communications has the largest Lerner Index for loans and the largest (least negative) index for securities investments.

6. Conclusions

In this chapter, we studied the Lerner Index of monopoly power and estimated a multi-product Lerner Index for Chinese banks. The Lerner Index measures the percent markup of price over marginal cost and equals zero when price equals marginal cost. Higher values of the Lerner Index indicate greater monopoly power. Banks in China are dominated by state-owned commercial banks (SOCBs) and are subject to price controls which set minimum interest rates that banks can charge on loans and maximum interest rates that they can pay for deposits. Because market prices are either distorted by price controls or non-existent, our method recovers shadow prices for the various outputs produced (loans and investments) such that the output prices are consistent with banks having chosen outputs and inputs so as to maximize profits. Prices are estimated from a translog input distance function, marginal cost is estimated from a translog cost function, and both functions are estimated using stochastic frontier analysis.

Individual output Lerner Indexes are estimated for net loans and securities investments, holding fee income earned constant. A consistently aggregated Lerner Index is derived by weighting each individual Lerner Index by its share of shadow revenue. Net loans make up approximately 90% of bank shadow revenues and investments 10%. Estimates of the Lerner Index indicate that Chinese SOCBs have monopoly power in loans and the markup of price over marginal cost is about 48%. In addition, Chinese SOCBs overproduce securities investments, possibly due to liquidity concerns and risk-based capital requirements.

As of 2019, the four largest Chinese state-owned banks were the largest in the world in terms of total assets, but their large size may be fleeting. In

1970, the US had the ten largest banks in the world, but by 1992, Japan was home to eight of the ten largest banks (Fukuyama *et al.*, 1997). Like their US and Japanese counterparts, Chinese banks face a net regulatory burden.[9] Regulatory reforms that liberalize prices might help induce competition in Chinese financial services and reduce monopoly power among state-owned commercial banks.

---

[9] See Saunders *et al.* (2021) for discussion on the net regulatory burden.

Chapter 7

Estimation and Application of Lerner-Type Indexes for the Public Sector: German Theatres

Kristina Bishop*, **Rolf G. Färe**[†], **Shawna Grosskopf**[†], **Kathy Hayes***,
Bill Weber[‡], **and Heike Wetzel**[§]

Department of Economics, Southern Methodist University, Dallas, USA
[†]*Department of Economics, Oregon State University, Corvallis, USA*
[‡]*Department of Accounting, Economics and Finance,*
Southeast Missouri State University, Cape Girardeau, USA
[§]*Institute of Economics, University of Kassel, Kassel, Germany*

1. Introduction

When governments consider outsourcing or privatizing some of their activities, it would be useful to compare the (shadow) output prices to their marginal costs via a measure of market power as summarized by the Lerner Index.[1] If market power exists, i.e., the output price exceeds the marginal cost for the given service, outsourcing or privatization may drive down the output price toward marginal cost and obtain a "competitive" equilibrium situation. Negative values of the Lerner Index — price less than marginal cost — might occur when various interest groups capture some part of government to expand those services beyond the competitive equilibrium. This chapter provides a model to estimate the generally unknown price of public services as well as marginal costs. Given the data generally available from the public sector, i.e., input and output quantities and input prices, we employ two functions: the cost function and Shephard's (1953) input distance function.

---

[1]Lerner (1934).

The data required for estimating these two functions include those mentioned above: input quantities and prices and output quantities. Noting that input quantities times their prices yields total cost, we have the final piece of data required. Output prices are considered to be unknown or possibly unreliable; however, we show that shadow output prices may be retrieved by appealing to a duality theorem between the input distance function and the profit function, which we shall show presently. See also Färe and Primont (1995: p. 129).

We offer an application of our approach using an unbalanced panel of 1791 observations on German public theatres for the 2004–2005 to 2017–2018 theatrical seasons.

2. Past Research

In their classic book, *Public Finance in Theory and Practice*, Musgrave and Musgrave (1980) argue that when consumers demand public or social goods government must step in to provide such goods. They write (p. 3) "The problem, then, is how the government should determine how much of such goods is to be provided." Their theory of allocation views public servants as enlightened and benevolent actors whose goal is to allocate resources so as to maximize societal welfare. In contrast, Brennan and Buchanan (1980) posit that government might also be modeled as Leviathan, with its agents seeking to extract taxes and provide services that maximize their own utility, rather than any enlightened notion of social welfare. Such behavior can persist when government has monopoly power in the provision of services. If, however, local governments compete for mobile citizens (Tiebout, 1956), the monopoly behavior can be limited, with the resulting tax and expenditure package approximating a competitive equilibrium. Similar to Tiebout (1956), Brennan and Buchanan (1980) argue that Leviathan's appetite can be limited by suitable dispersion of authority among many local governments. However, McKenzie and Staaf (1978) and Grossman (1989) argue that revenue sharing and intergovernmental grants allow government agents to collude, resulting in a monopoly outcome. Caplan (2001) argues that when property taxes are completely capitalized into land prices, local governments can stifle competition since mobile landlords would pay the entire burden of excessive taxes via lower land prices.

Our goal in this chapter is not to take sides in the debate over enlightened versus self-serving government agents; surely there are some of both. Instead, in the following section, we provide a method for testing for non-optimal outcomes even when prices of government outputs are unavailable or uninformative. To our knowledge, ours is the first application of the shadow-price Lerner Index applied to services provided by the public sector.

Our application examines German public theatres. In 2015, spending on recreation, culture and religion averaged 1% of GDP in OECD countries (OECD General Government Spending). So, even though the public spending on theatres is less than 1%, during times of fiscal stress, this kind of discretionary spending might be one area where governments might look to enhance efficiency via privatization.

Baumol (1967) argued that productivity growth is slow in labor intensive industries, such as those found in the public provision of education and the arts, and that these industries will experience a cost disease as salaries in the industry must rise to match those in more productive industries. One strand of research on the economics of theatres and other cultural endeavours has examined the efficiency and productivity of these endeavours. Gapinski (1984) estimated demand and production functions for the Royal Shakespeare Company and found that the theatres overproduce relative to a profit maximizing output but that the government subsidy to theatres is less than the increase in consumer surplus from overproduction. Zieba (2011) analyzed the efficiency of Austrian and Swiss non-profit theatres and found that subsidies and competition reduce the variance in efficiency across theatres. Last and Wetzel (2010) controlled for subsidies as a quasi-fixed factor in their estimates of translog cost and input distance functions for German theatres and found some evidence of inefficiency. Their estimates were extended by Last and Wetzel (2011) to calculate a Malmquist productivity index in which they found support for Baumol's cost disease. Zieba and Newman (2013) also examine efficiency of both private and public German theatres and found that reunification between East and West Germany helped enhance efficiency among theatres via greater competition. Fazioli and Filippini (1997) estimate a theatre cost function and find evidence of both scale and scope economies. Neligan (2006) examines the correlates of a conventionality index for German public theatres during the 1998–1999 theatrical season. The conventionality index equals the average number of times a play is shown, with higher values indicating greater conventionality (or less diversity). The findings indicate that a larger subsidy reduces conventionality as theatres provide a more diverse offering of plays.

Taalas (1997) finds that Finnish theatres have costs that are about 5% higher than necessary to produce a given output. Furthermore, Taalas finds a capital-using bias among theatres; as output expands, theatres increase auditorium size rather than using labor more intensively to stage reruns of existing shows. Castiglione *et al.* (2018) find that Italian performing arts companies with between 10 and 49 workers are more scale efficient than companies larger than 49 workers or less than 10 workers. Fernández-Blanco *et al.* (2018) estimate an input distance function for performing arts companies operating in municipal theatres in Warsaw. Here, the authors find that technical inefficiencies average about 7% and find evidence of Baumol's cost disease, as theatres became more inefficient over time. However, the authors also find that a higher government subsidy leads to improvements in quality and diversity, i.e., novelty in the number of productions offered can enhance efficiency. Frey (1997) argues that festivals, as a venue for performing arts, have been able to overcome Baumol's cost disease as they make use of existing auditoriums and volunteer labor.

3. Theoretical Underpinnings

Here we develop the theory used to determine public sector market power when market output prices are unknown. We can retrieve marginal costs from the cost function by evaluating the gradient vector with respect to output quantity of the estimated cost function. Let $y \in R_+^M$ denote output quantities and $w \in R_+^N$ an input price vector with $x \in R_+^N$ a vector of input quantities. The technology set is defined as the set of inputs and outputs such that the inputs can produce the outputs, i.e.,

$$T = \{(x, y): \ x \text{ can produce } y\} \tag{1}$$

The technology can also be represented by the input requirement set which is defined as

$$L(y) = \{x : x \text{ can produce } y\} \tag{2}$$

This set models all inputs that can produce the observed output vector y.[2] Given the input requirement set and input prices, the cost function is defined as

$$C(y, w) = \min_x \{wx : x \in L(y)\} \tag{3}$$

Here we assume that the minimum exists; for a discussion, see Färe and Primont (1995). The cost function is homogeneous of degree $+1$ in input prices, which we exploit in specifying a parametric form for $C(y, w)$. In particular, a homogeneous function that is also a flexible functional form (or generalized quadratic) can only take two forms: (1) the mean of order ρ and (2) the translog (see Färe and Sung, 1986). Since the latter includes both first- and second-order parameters, it is our preferred functional form.

Shephard's (1953) input distance function is the second function required to construct our Lerner Index when output price data are unavailable. Like the cost function, the input distance function is defined in terms of the input requirement sets:

$$D_i(y, x) = \max_\lambda \{\lambda : (x/\lambda) \in L(y)\} \tag{4}$$

i.e., it seeks the largest feasible radial contraction of the observed input vector.[3] Under mild conditions, this function represents the input requirement set

$$D_i(y, x) \geq 1 \quad \text{if and only if } x \in L(y) \tag{5}$$

In addition, it is homogeneous in the input quantities

$$D_i(y, \lambda x) = \lambda D_i(y, x) \tag{6}$$

which follows from its definition. As with the cost function, the homogeneity property of the distance function makes the translog our preferred parameterization.

---

[2]For an axiomatic representation of $L(y)$, see, e.g., Färe and Primont (1995: p. 129).
[3]Note that for $x \notin L(y)$, it is defined as the smallest radial expansion of x.

Next consider the case in which a single output is produced; then the Lerner Index is given by

$$L = \frac{p - dC(y, w)/dy}{p}$$

$$L = \frac{p - MC}{p} \tag{7}$$

where p is the output price and $dC(y, w)/dy = MC$ is the marginal cost of producing the single output y. Under perfect competition, $p = MC$ and $L = 0$.

In the more realistic case that multiple outputs are produced, following Baumol *et al.* (1982), the indexes are defined individually, i.e.,

$$L_m = \frac{p_m - \partial C(y, w)/\partial y_m}{p_m}, \quad m = 1, \ldots, M \tag{8}$$

Our next task is to identify and estimate the unknown (shadow) prices of the outputs y_m, $m = 1, \ldots, M$. For this we need to introduce the profit function which we specify in terms of the input distance function, following a duality result found in Färe and Primont (1995). Let $p \in R_+^M$ be a vector of output prices, $w \in R_+^N$ a vector of input prices, and denote output quantities by $y \in R_+^M$ and input quantities $x \in R_+^N$. Noting that if $(x, y) \in T$, then $x \in L(y)$ and we may write the profit function as

$$\pi(w, p) = \max_{x,y} \; py - wx, \quad \text{s.t. } x \in L(y) \tag{9}$$

where py is the revenue, wx is the cost and their difference is profit. The solution to problem (9) seeks maximum profit by choosing optimal quantities of outputs and inputs.

Specifically the profit function $\pi(w, p)$ in (9) seeks the maximum feasible difference between py and wx given $x \in L(y)$. Next we bring in the input distance function. Recalling that

$$x \in L(y) \quad \Longleftrightarrow \quad D_i(y, x) \geq 1 \tag{10}$$

we may formulate one part of the duality theorem between the profit function and the input distance function,[4] namely

$$\pi(w, p) = \max_{x,y} \, py - \frac{wx}{D_i(y, x)} \tag{11}$$

i.e., the profit function can be derived by maximizing the difference between revenue py and the (observed) cost normalized by the input distance function, $\frac{wx}{D_i(y,x)}$.

The first-order condition associated with the profit maximization problem (11) yields the shadow prices we seek, namely

$$p + \frac{wx}{D_i(y, x)^2} \, \nabla_y \, D_i(y, x) = 0 \tag{12}$$

or

$$p_m = -\frac{wx}{D_i(y, x)^2} \partial D_i(y, x)/\partial y_m, \quad m = 1, \ldots, M \tag{13}$$

These shadow prices require that we estimate an input distance function in order to solve for the gradient vector in (12).

Having derived a shadow price p_m for each output $m = 1, \ldots, M$ as well as the marginal costs $\partial C(y, w)/\partial y_m$, $m = 1, \ldots, M$, we may also ask the following: What is the overall Lerner Index when there are multiple outputs?

Using what we call the "denominator rule",[5] one may construct an aggregate index as follows. Let the weights for the Lerner Index for each output be value shares, see (19), s_m, $m = 1, \ldots, M$, with $\sum_{m=1}^{M} s_m = 1$.

---

[4]The second half of the duality is the retrieval of the distance function from the profit function, i.e.,

$$D_i(y, x) = \inf_{w,p} \left\{ \frac{wx}{py - \pi(w, p)} \right\}$$

For details, see Färe and Primont (1995: p. 129).

[5]See Färe and Karagiannis (2017). Using value shares as weights was suggested to us in a conversation with W.E. Diewert.

Then, it follows that the aggregated index takes the form

$$L = \sum_{m=1}^{M} s_m \frac{p_m - \partial C(y, w)/\partial y_m}{p_m} \tag{14}$$

Note that the Lerner Index for output m can be written as

$$L_m = \frac{p_m - \mathrm{MC}_m}{p_m} \left(\frac{y_m}{y_m}\right), \quad m = 1, \ldots, M \tag{15}$$

Consider the ratio, I, written as

$$I = \frac{\sum_{m=1}^{M} y_m (p_m - \mathrm{MC}_m)}{\sum_{m=1}^{M} p_m y_m} \tag{16}$$

This ratio has the property that $I = 0$ when $p_m = \mathrm{MC}_m$, $m = 1, \ldots, M$, and $I = 1$ when $\mathrm{MC}_m = 0$, $m = 1, \ldots, M$, just like the aggregate Lerner Index in (14). Furthermore, write I as

$$I = \sum_{m=1}^{M} \frac{y_m (p_m - \mathrm{MC}_m)}{\sum_{m=1}^{M} p_m y_m} \frac{p_m}{p_m} \tag{17}$$

and then rearrange to get

$$I = \sum_{m=1}^{M} \frac{p_m y_m \left(\frac{p_m - \mathrm{MC}_m}{p_m}\right)}{\sum_{m=1}^{M} p_m y_m}$$

$$= \sum_{m=1}^{M} \frac{p_m y_m (L_m)}{\sum_{m=1}^{M} p_m y_m} \tag{18}$$

Thus, the ratio I equals the aggregate Lerner Index (14) when the weights are chosen to equal the value shares of shadow revenues:

$$s_m = \frac{p_m y_m}{\sum_{m=1}^{M} p_m y_m}, \quad m = 1, \ldots, M \tag{19}$$

We use these value share weights in our empirical example.

4. Translog Cost and Distance Functions

We apply the Lerner Index using an unbalanced panel of German theatres during the 14 theatrical seasons from 2004–2005 to 2017–2018. We use the translog functional form to estimate both the input distance function and the cost function using the Aigner and Chu (1968) deterministic method. We also control for other exogenous variables that might impact theatre efficiency or costs of production. These exogenous variables are represented by $z = (z_1, \ldots, z_J)$. In addition, we add $T - 1$ time indicator variables, DT^t, to control for time effects common to all theatres. In the empirical section, we discuss these exogenous variables in more detail.

The translog input distance function takes the form

$$
\ln D_i(y, x) = \alpha_0 + \sum_{m=1}^{M} \alpha_m \ln y_m + 0.5 \sum_{m=1}^{M} \sum_{m'=1}^{M} \alpha_{mm'} \ln y_m \ln y_{m'} + \sum_{n=1}^{N} \beta_n \ln x_n
$$

$$
+ 0.5 \sum_{n=1}^{N} \sum_{n'=1}^{N} \beta_{nn} \ln x_n \ln x_{n'} + \sum_{m=1}^{M} \sum_{n=1}^{N} \delta_{mn} \ln x_n \ln y_m
$$

$$
+ \sum_{j=1}^{J} \psi_j z_j \sum_{t=2}^{T} f_t DT_t \tag{20}
$$

The translog cost function takes the form

$$
\ln C(y, w) = \alpha_0 + \sum_{m=1}^{M} a_m \ln y_m + 0.5 \sum_{m=1}^{M} \sum_{m'=1}^{M} a_{mm'} \ln y_m \ln y_{m'} + \sum_{n=1}^{N} b_n \ln w_n
$$

$$
+ 0.5 \sum_{n=1}^{N} \sum_{n'=1}^{N} b_{nn} \ln w_n \ln w_{n'} + \sum_{m=1}^{M} \sum_{n=1}^{N} d_{mn} \ln y_m \ln w_n
$$

$$
+ \sum_{j=1}^{J} e_j z_j \sum_{t=2}^{T} f_t DT_t \tag{21}
$$

We follow Aigner-Chu (1968) and use a deterministic method to estimate each function. For the input distance function, we choose parameters $(\alpha_0, \alpha_m, \alpha_{mm'}, \beta_n, \beta_{nn'}, \delta_{mn}, \psi_j, f_t)$ to minimize the radial distance of the observed inputs to the isoquant frontier. In addition, we impose feasibility, homogeneity, monotonicity and symmetry conditions on the parameter estimates. Appending a k superscript to the inputs and outputs in (20), the linear programming problem is solved for all time periods as:

$$\underset{a_0,a_m,a_{mm},\beta_n,\beta_{nn},\delta_{mn},\psi_j,f_t}{\text{minimize}} \sum_{k=1}^{K} \ln D_i(y^k, x^k) \text{ subject to}$$

(i) $\ln D_i(y^k, x^k) \geq 0, \ k = 1, \ldots, K$

(ii) $\sum_{n=1}^{N} \beta_n = 1, \ \sum_{n'=1}^{N} \beta_{nn'} = 0, \ n = 1, \ldots, N \ \sum_{m=1}^{M} \delta_{mn} = 0, \ n = 1, \ldots, N$

(iii) $\dfrac{\partial \ln D_i(y^k, x^k)}{\partial \ln x_n^k} = \beta_n + \sum_{n'=1}^{N} \beta_{nn'} \ln x_{n'}^k + \sum_{m=1}^{M} \delta_{mn} \ln y_m^k \geq 0$

$$n = 1, \ldots, N, \ k = 1, \ldots, K$$

(iv) $\dfrac{\partial \ln D_i(y^k, x^k)}{\partial \ln y_m^k} = \alpha_m + \sum_{m'=1}^{M} \alpha_{mm'} \ln y_{m'}^k + \sum_{n=1}^{N} \delta_{mn} \ln x_n^k \leq 0$

$$m = 1, \ldots, M, \ k = 1, \ldots, K$$

(v) $\beta_{nn'} = \beta_{n'n}, \ n \neq n', \ \alpha_{mm'} = \alpha_{m'm}, \ m \neq m'$ \hfill (22)

The restriction (22(i)) imposes feasibility for each of the $k = 1, \ldots, K$ decision-making units (DMUs). In (22(ii)), the distance function is restricted to be homogenous of degree 1. The restrictions in (22(iii) and (iv)) impose monotoncity conditions and finally, symmetry conditions are imposed in (22(v)).

The cost function is also estimated using the Aigner–Chu deterministic method by choosing parameters $(a_0, a_m, a_{mm}, b_n, b_{nn}, d_{mn}, e_j, f_t)$ of the cost function to minimize the deviation between actual costs and minimum costs of production. The linear programming problem we solve to estimate the cost function parameters is

$$\underset{a_0,a_m,a_{mm},b_n,b_{nn},d_{mn},e_j,f_t}{\min} \sum_{k=1}^{K} (\ln c_k - \ln c(w^{kt}, y^{kt})) \text{ s.t.}$$

(i) $\ln C(w^{kt}, y^{kt}, z^k) \leq \ln c^k, \ k = 1, \ldots, K$

(ii) $\sum_{n=1}^{N} b_n = 1, \ \sum_{n'=1}^{N} b_{nn'} = 0, \ n = 1, \ldots, N \ \sum_{m=1}^{M} d_{mn} = 0, \ n = 1, \ldots, N$

(iii) $\dfrac{\partial \ln C(w^{kt}, y^{kt})}{\partial \ln w_n^k} = b_n + \displaystyle\sum_{n'=1}^{N} b_{nn'} \ln w_{n'}^k + \sum_{m=1}^{M} d_{mn} \ln y_m^k \geq 0, \ n = 1, \ldots, N$

$\qquad k = 1, \ldots, K, t = 1, \ldots, T$

(iv) $\dfrac{\partial \ln C(w^{kt}, y^{kt}, z^k)}{\partial \ln y_m^k} = a_m + \displaystyle\sum_{m'=1}^{M} a_{mm'} \ln y_{m'}^k + \sum_{n=1}^{N} \delta_{mn} \ln w_n^k \geq 0, \ m = 1, \ldots, M$

$\qquad k = 1, \ldots, K, t = 1, \ldots, T$

(v) $b_{nn'} = b_{n'n}, \ n \neq n', \ a_{mm'} = a_{m'm}, \ m \neq m'$ \hfill (23)

The restrictions in (23) impose feasibility (i), homogeneity (ii), monotonicity (iii and iv) and symmetry conditions (v) on the translog cost function.

For ease of exposition we drop the k superscripts. The shadow prices of the outputs are

$$p_m = -\frac{wx}{D_i(y, x)^2} \cdot \frac{\partial D_i(y, x)}{\partial y_m}, \quad m = 1, \ldots, M \qquad (24)$$

and noting that

$$\frac{\partial D_i(y, x)}{\partial y_m} = \frac{\partial \ln D_i(y, x)}{\partial \ln y_m} \cdot \frac{D_i(y, x)}{y_m}, \quad m = 1, \ldots, M \qquad (25)$$

we find the shadow price of the output from the translog function (20) as

$$p_m = -\frac{wx}{D_i(y, x)} \left(\frac{a_m + \sum_{m'=1}^{M} a_{mm'} \ln y_{m'} + \sum_{n=1}^{N} \delta_{mn} \ln x_n}{y_m} \right),$$
$$m = 1, \ldots, M$$

$$(26)$$

The marginal cost of output is

$$\frac{\partial C(y, w)}{\partial y_m} = \frac{\partial \ln c}{\partial \ln y_m} \cdot \frac{c}{y_m}, \quad m = 1, \ldots, M \qquad (27)$$

Using the translog cost function (21), marginal cost is

$$\frac{\partial C(y, w)}{\partial y_m} = \left(c_m + \sum_{m'=1}^{M} c_{mm'} \ln y_{m'} + \sum_{n=1}^{N} d_{mn} \ln w_n \right) \left(\frac{c}{y_m} \right),$$
$$m = 1, \ldots, M$$

$$(28)$$

Table 1. Descriptive Statistics

Variable	Mean	Std. Dev.	Minimum	Maximum
Spectators y_1	140807	105752	423	636187
Performances y_2	486	249	5	1618
Artistic staff x_1	134	104	1	679
Admin/technical staff x_2	152	132	2	877
Operating expenditures x_3	5319999	5522925	97439	43101784
w_1	54463	43217	3959	966011
w_2	42078	10275	7501	80975
w_3	1	0	1	1
Venues z_1	6	3	1	25
Subsidy	13319808	9813564	218452	56019305
Cost $= wx$	20010659	18097976	444563.9	125938746

Thus, the Lerner Index for output m can be derived by substituting (26) and (28) into (15).

5. The Empirics

The unbalanced panel data on German theatres are for the 2004–2005 to 2017–2018 theatrical seasons. We assume that theatres use artistic staff (x_1), administrative/technical staff (x_2) and non-labor operating expenses (x_3) to produce two outputs — spectators (y_1) and performances (y_2). We also controlled for the number of venues (z_1) that each theatre maintained.[6] The prices of artistic and administrative/technical staff equal the ratio of payroll for each type of staff to the number of staff.

Table 1 reports descriptive statistics for the pooled data. The average number of spectators attending performances in a theatrical season is 141 thousand and average performances per season equal 486 per theatre. The number of spectators varies from 423 to more than 600,000 and theatre

---

[6]We tested various model specifications regarding which control variables to include. These models were as follows: 1. no controls, 2. # of venues as a control, 3. amount of subsidy as a control and 4. subsidies and venues as controls. Using the Kolmogorov–Smirnov test for differences in two empirical distribution functions, we found significant differences between the technical efficiency estimates for 1 vs. 2, 1 vs. 3, and 1 vs. 4, but no difference in estimates for 2 vs. 4. Therefore, since controlling for the number of venues gives the same empirical distribution of input technical efficiency as controlling for both venues and the subsidy, we opt for the more parsimonious model that includes only venues as a control.

performances vary from 5 to 1618 per season. On average, there were 134 artistic staff and 152 administrative/technical staff per theatre. Average artistic staff salaries were 54 thousand Euros and administrative/technical staff salaries were 42 thousand Euros. Operating expenses averaged 5.3 million Euros. The average number of venues a theatre maintains was 6 and ranges from 1 to 25. We estimated two models controlling for the number of venues a theatre maintains. In model A, venues (z_1) enter the translog cost and input distance functions in log form ($\ln z_1$ Model A) and in model B, venues enter the two functions in level form (z_1 Model B). Theatres also received an average subsidy of 13.3 million Euros.[7] The total cost of employing artistic staff, administrative and technical staff, and other operating expenses averages 20 million Euros per theatre with a range between 445 thousand Euros and 126 million Euros.

The translog input distance function estimates for the two models are reported in Table 2 and the translog cost function estimates are reported in Table 3. Table 4 reports the parameter estimates of the time indicator variables for the translog cost and input distance functions. To avoid exact linear dependence, the indicator variable for the 2004–2005 season was dropped in both functions. A positive time coefficient in the input distance function for any of the seasons after 2004–2005 indicates that an observation of input and output quantities was further from the technological frontier in the particular season than that same observation would have been relative to the 2004–2005 technological frontier. Thus, positive (negative) time coefficients in the input distance function indicate technological progress (regress). Similarly, a negative time coefficient in the cost function indicates that the cost of producing a given level of output, input prices held constant, is less in the particular season relative to 2004–2005. Therefore, negative (positive) time coefficients in the cost function indicate technological progress (regress).

For the translog input distance function, models A and B both estimate positive time coefficients with similar magnitudes in every year, indicating technological progress relative to the 2004–2005 season. For the translog cost function, models A and B both estimate negative time coefficients of similar magnitude and are consistent with the input distance function

---

[7]All money values have been deflated by the consumer price index for Germany (Statisches Bundesamt — Federal Statistical Office) with a base year of 2015.

Table 2. Translog Input Distance Function Parameter Estimates

Parameter	Variable	Model A Estimate	Model B Estimate
α_0	1	8.607	1.833
α_1	$\ln y_1$	−0.509	0.029
α_2	$\ln y_2$	−0.129	−0.040
α_{11}	$\ln y_1^2$	−0.022	−0.024
α_{12}	$\ln y_1 \ln y_2$	−0.011	−0.039
α_{22}	$\ln y_2^2$	0.018	0.058
β_1	$\ln x_1$	0.571	0.171
β_2	$\ln x_2$	1.246	1.049
β_3	$\ln x_3$	−0.817	−0.220
β_{11}	$\ln x_1^2$	0.030	0.018
β_{12}	$\ln x_1 \ln x_2$	−0.003	−0.013
β_{13}	$\ln x_1 \ln x_3$	−0.027	−0.005
β_{22}	$\ln x_2^2$	0.142	0.157
β_{23}	$\ln x_2 \ln x_3$	−0.139	−0.145
β_{33}	$\ln x_3^2$	0.166	0.150
δ_{11}	$\ln y_1 \ln x_1$	−0.022	−0.024
δ_{12}	$\ln y_1 \ln x_2$	0.063	0.094
δ_{13}	$\ln y_1 \ln x_3$	−0.041	−0.070
δ_{21}	$\ln y_2 \ln x_1$	0.010	0.038
δ_{22}	$\ln y_2 \ln x_2$	−0.020	−0.039
δ_{23}	$\ln y_2 \ln x_3$	0.010	0.001
ψ_1	$\ln z_1$	−0.141	.
ψ_1	z_1	.	−0.023

in indicating technological progress. For the input distance function, the positive time coefficients trend downward during the period, which indicates that the greatest inward shift in the isoquant occurred during 2005–2006 to 2015–2006, but during the last two seasons, the isoquant shifted back toward the 2004–2005 technology.

Table 5 reports the mean estimates of the input distance function and the number of frontier theatres for each model. Pooled mean efficiency for the two models are 0.51 with 22 and 23 frontier producers for the two models, respectively.

Average shadow prices, marginal costs and Lerner Indexes are reported in Tables 6 and 7. For model A, the value share weights for the aggregate Lerner Index average 0.97 for spectators and 0.03 for productions and are constant over the period. In model B, the value share weights average 0.9 for

Table 3. Translog Cost Function Estimates

Parameter	Variable	Model A Estimate	Model B Estimate
a_0	1	2.19751	−2.76227
a_1	$\ln y_1$	−0.4233	0.21301
a_2	$\ln y_2$	0.17561	−0.21092
a_{11}	$\ln y_1^2$	0.11471	0.06039
a_{12}	$\ln y_1 \ln y_2$	0.01057	0.03358
a_{22}	$\ln y_2^2$	0.00912	−0.0011
b_1	$\ln w_1$	0.81635	0.43812
b_2	$\ln w_2$	−0.2759	0.56188
b_3	$\ln w_3$	0.45954	0
b_{11}	$\ln w_1^2$	−0.04979	−0.0303
b_{12}	$\ln w_1 \ln w_2$	0.06875	0.0303
b_{13}	$\ln w_1 \ln w_3$	−0.01896	0
b_{22}	$\ln w_2^2$	−0.05619	−0.0303
b_{23}	$\ln w_2 \ln w_3$	−0.01256	0
b_{33}	$\ln w_3^2$	0.03152	0
d_{11}	$\ln y_1 \ln w_1$	−0.09622	−0.06234
d_{12}	$\ln y_1 \ln w_2$	0.11541	0.06234
d_{13}	$\ln y_1 \ln w_3$	−0.01919	0
d_{21}	$\ln y_2 \ln w_1$	0.04684	0.06841
d_{22}	$\ln y_2 \ln w_2$	−0.07134	−0.06841
d_{23}	$\ln y_2 \ln w_3$	0.02451	0
e_1	$\ln z_1$	0.20425	.
e_1	z_1	.	0.02644

spectators and 0.1 for performances and are also constant over the period. The last column in each table reports the aggregate share weighted Lerner Index.

In model A, the average price of spectators is 79.6 Euros and the marginal cost of a spectator is 67.5 Euros and the average Lerner Index for spectators is 0.15, indicating a markup of price over marginal cost of 15%. Performances have an average price of 907.3 Euros with a marginal cost of 2022 and an average Lerner Index of −1.58 which indicates that marginal cost exceeds price by 158%. Together, the results indicate that theatres are

Table 4. Time Indicator Estimates

Season	Parameter	Model A, $z = \ln(\text{Venues})$		Model B, $z = \text{Venues}$	
		$\ln D_i(y,x,z)$	$\ln c(y,w,z)$	$\ln D_i(y,x,z)$	$\ln c(y,w,z)$
2005–2006	f_2	0.331	−0.34	0.315	−0.3
2006–2007	f_3	0.271	−0.3	0.259	−0.27
2007–2008	f_4	0.21	−0.23	0.202	−0.19
2008–2009	f_5	0.309	−0.19	0.294	−0.21
2009–2010	f_6	0.144	−0.18	0.144	−0.15
2010–2011	f_7	0.237	−0.36	0.255	−0.34
2011–2012	f_8	0.216	−0.09	0.24	−0.06
2012–2013	f_9	0.228	−0.06	0.207	−0.07
2013–2014	f_{10}	0.082	−0.1	0.089	−0.06
2014–2015	f_{11}	0.342	−0.14	0.376	−0.17
2015–2016	f_{12}	0.169	−0.19	0.129	−0.14
2016–2017	f_{13}	0.078	−0.06	0.082	−0.06
2017–2018	f_{14}	0.084	−0.05	0.093	−0.05

Table 5. Efficiency Estimates

Year	K	Model A		Model B	
		$\frac{1}{D_i(y,x)}$	Theatres on Frontier	$\frac{1}{D_i(y,x)}$	Theatres on Frontier
2004–2005	132	0.56	2	0.55	2
2005–2006	117	0.47	2	0.48	1
2006–2007	124	0.50	2	0.51	2
2007–2008	124	0.53	1	0.54	1
2008–2009	124	0.48	1	0.49	1
2009–2010	125	0.55	1	0.55	2
2010–2011	127	0.50	2	0.50	2
2011–2012	129	0.50	1	0.48	1
2012–2013	130	0.49	1	0.50	1
2013–2014	130	0.57	3	0.56	3
2014–2015	131	0.44	1	0.43	1
2015–2016	132	0.52	1	0.54	2
2016–2017	132	0.56	2	0.55	2
2017–2018	134	0.53	2	0.52	2
All years	1791	0.51	22	0.51	23

Table 6. Shadow Prices, Marginal Costs and Lerner Indexes, Model A

Season	Spectators			Performances			
	p_1	MC_1	L_1	p_2	MC_2	L_2	L_{agg}
2004–2005	105.1	91.6	0.13	1099.2	2626	−1.79	0.08
2005–2006	72.1	55.2	0.23	927.1	1821.7	−1.17	0.19
2006–2007	74.6	57	0.24	898.1	1785.5	−1.13	0.20
2007–2008	78.4	61	0.23	946.4	1911.8	−1.23	0.19
2008–2009	71.4	65	0.10	866	2086.1	−1.67	0.05
2009–2010	83.7	65	0.23	986.4	2011.2	−1.23	0.19
2010–2011	76.4	55.1	0.28	855.1	1644.6	−1.36	0.24
2011–2012	75.9	70.3	0.08	846.8	2084.1	−2.13	0.03
2012–2013	74.9	72.1	0.04	854.5	2149.4	−1.93	−0.01
2013–2014	86	70.1	0.19	964.6	2083.6	−1.47	0.14
2014–2015	66.8	68.1	−0.02	740.7	1987.2	−2.43	−0.07
2015–2016	77.8	63.9	0.18	862.3	1856.3	−1.55	0.13
2016–2017	85.5	73.6	0.14	932.2	2109.1	−1.57	0.09
2017–2018	83.8	74	0.11	924.3	2099.2	−1.68	0.07
Pooled	79.6	67.5	0.15	907.3	2022.0	−1.58	0.11

Table 7. Shadow Prices, Marginal Costs and Lerner Indexes, Model B

Season	Spectators			Performances			
	p_1	MC_1	L_1	p_2	MC_2	L_2	L_{agg}
2004–2005	100.6	84.8	0.142	3813	4771.4	−0.323	0.10
2005–2006	70.2	52.8	0.234	3049.2	3310.2	−0.136	0.20
2006–2007	72.6	54.4	0.243	2971	3233.5	−0.121	0.21
2007–2008	76	58.5	0.226	3133.8	3471.8	−0.167	0.19
2008–2009	69.7	58.5	0.155	2937	3585	−0.275	0.12
2009–2010	80.3	61.8	0.226	3269.8	3669.9	−0.173	0.19
2010–2011	72.6	52.3	0.27	2846.1	3013.4	−0.126	0.24
2011–2012	71.4	67.6	0.044	2765.8	3840.1	−0.489	−0.00
2012–2013	73.5	66.1	0.086	2895.2	3791	−0.387	0.05
2013–2014	81.9	67.4	0.162	3212.6	3882.5	−0.276	0.12
2014–2015	61.8	61	−0.004	2385.1	3466.4	−0.558	−0.05
2015–2016	77.5	62.4	0.182	2991.7	3539.2	−0.242	0.15
2016–2017	81.6	68.1	0.149	3110.5	3832.9	−0.296	0.11
2017–2018	79.4	68.4	0.118	3072.3	3863.3	−0.35	0.08
Pooled	76.5	63.3	0.16	3032.9	3669.7	−0.28	0.12

giving too many performances and attracting too few spectators. The Lerner Index for spectators is positive for every season except 2014–2015 and the Lerner Index for performances is negative for every theatrical season.

The model B results are reported in Table 7. The average price and marginal cost of spectators are about 3 and 4 Euros less in model B than in model A. However, the average price and marginal cost of performances are higher in model B than in model A. The two models give similar signs for the two Lerner Indexes: positive for spectators and negative for performances.

Trend lines in the mean Lerner Indexes for spectators, performances and the aggregate Lerner Index for the two models are shown in Figure 1. For model A, the average Lerner Index for spectators is positive in every year except 2014–2015 and averages 0.15 for the pooled sample, indicating that the markup is about 15% of price. The average Lerner Index for performances is negative in every year which indicates that theatres are overproducing performances relative to the competitive equilibrium. The aggregate Lerner Index ranges from −0.07 in 2014–2015 to 0.24 in 2010–2011.

For model B, also shown in Figure 1, the Lerner Index for spectators is positive in every year except 2014–2015, with a slightly higher pooled mean ($L_1 = 0.16$) relative to model A ($L_1 = 0.15$). Similar to model A, the Lerner Index for performances is negative in every year but has pooled mean of $L_2 = -0.28$ compared to model A with $L_2 = -1.58$. Finally, for model B, the aggregate mean Lerner Index ranges from −0.05 in 2014–2015 to 0.24 in 2010–2011 with a pooled mean of $L = 0.12$.

Table 8 reports counts of the number of theatres with positive/negative Lerner Indexes for the two models. Several theatres in each model have a price for performances equal to zero resulting in undefined Lerner Index for performances. For model A, 1444 theatres priced spectators greater than marginal cost resulting in $L_1 > 0$ and 347 theatres priced spectators at less than marginal cost resulting in $L_1 < 0$. For performances, only 13 theatres had prices greater than marginal cost while 1771 theatres had prices less than marginal cost. Seven theatres had performance prices equal to zero, which gave an undefined Lerner Index. A similar pattern exists for spectator and performances in model B where 1443 theatres had spectator prices greater than marginal cost and 348 theatres had spectator prices less than marginal cost, whereas 397 theatre had performance prices greater than

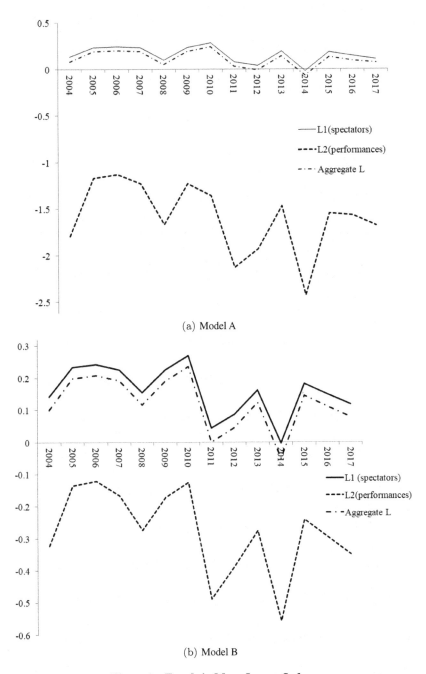

(a) Model A

(b) Model B

Figure 1. Trends in Mean Lerner Index

Table 8. Number of Theatres with Positive/Negative Lerner Indexes

Model A	Theatres with			
	$L_1 > 0$	$L_1 < 0$	L_1 undefined	Sum
$L_2 > 0$	11	2	0	13
$L_2 < 0$	1431	340	0	1771
L_2 undefined	2	5	0	7
Sum	1444	347	0	1791

Model B	Theatres with			
	$L_1 > 0$	$L_1 < 0$	L_1 undefined	Sum
$L_2 > 0$	372	25	0	397
$L_2 < 0$	1069	323	0	1392
L_2 undefined	2	0	0	2
Sum	1443	348	0	1791

marginal cost while 1392 theatre had spectator prices less than marginal cost.

The results in Table 8 indicate that in model A, the most common outcome was that 1431 theatres had monopoly power in both spectators and performances, whereas only 340 theatres produced too many spectators and too many performances relative to a competitive equilibrium. In model B, the most common outcome was that 1069 theatres had monopoly power in spectators but overproduced performances. In contrast to model A, where only 11 theatres exhibited monopoly power in both spectators and performances, the results of model B found that 372 theatres had monopoly power in both spectators and performances.

Figures 2–4 plot the Lerner Indexes for the two models against the subsidy received by each theatre. The subsidy and Lerner Index for spectators are negatively correlated, $r = -0.73$ for model A and $r = -0.01$ in model B. There is a small positive correlation between the subsidy and the Lerner Index for performances in model A, $r = 0.03$, but a negative correlation between subsidy and Lerner Index for performances, $r = -0.11$ in model B. Both models exhibit a negative correlation between the subsidy and the aggregate Lerner Index, $r = -0.35$ for model A and $r = -0.06$ for model B.

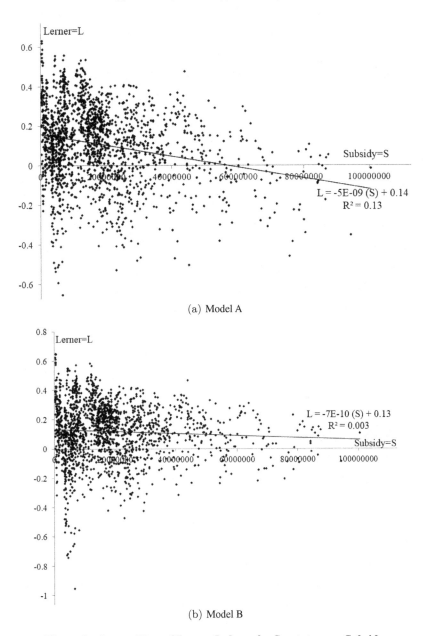

(a) Model A

(b) Model B

Figure 2. Scatter Plots of Lerner Indexes for Spectators vs. Subsidy

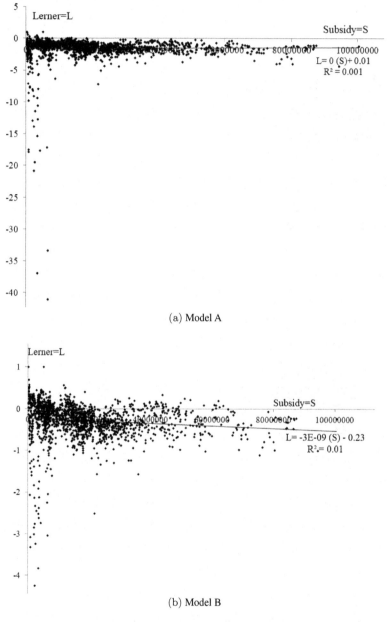

(a) Model A

(b) Model B

Figure 3.   Scatter Plots of Lerner Indexes for Performances vs. Subsidy

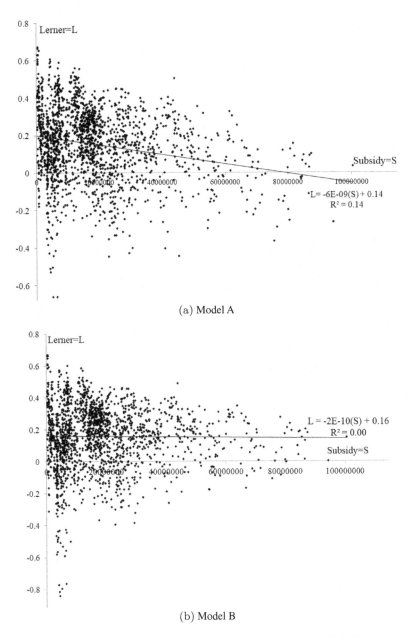

(a) Model A

(b) Model B

Figure 4. Scatter Plots of Aggregate Lerner Indexes vs. Subsidy

6. Conclusions

In this chapter, we investigated the degree of monopoly power held by German public theatres in their production of theatre performances and spectators. Since the prices of public sector outputs are often distorted by a lack of competition or by administrated prices, we exploited a duality between the input distance function and the profit function to estimate absolute shadow prices for outputs and compared those prices with marginal costs of production in individual product Lerner Indexes and a consistently aggregated Lerner Index. The Lerner Index gives the percentage markup of price over marginal cost, with a higher Lerner Index indicative of greater monopoly power.

Public theatres produce performances and spectators using artistic staff, administrative/technical staff and other operating expenditures. We control for time effects that are constant across theatres and allow for the number of venues a theatre operates to affect their technology. Using an unbalanced panel of 1791 German public theatres during the 14 seasons from 2004–2005 to 2017–2018, we find that German public theatres have monopoly power in spectators but overproduce performances. Thus, theatres that offer fewer performances but with more spectators per performance would improve efficiency. We also find that public subsidies, which account for approximately 90% of theatre expenditures, are inversely related to the amount of monopoly power accruing to theatres. Thus, subsidies appear to reduce monopoly power.

References

Aghion, P., Bloom, N., Blundell, R., Griffith, R., and Howitt, P. (2005). Competition and innovation: An inverted-U relationship. *Quarterly Journal of Economics*, 120(2), 701–728.

Agoraki, M.-E.K., Delis, M.D., and Pasiouras, F. (2011). Regulations, competition and bank risk-taking in transition countries. *Journal of Financial Stability*, 7, 38–48.

Aigner, D.J. and Chu, S.-F. (1968). On estimating the industry production function. *American Economic Review*, 58(4), 826–839.

Aigner, D.J., Lovell, C.A.K., and Schmidt, P. (1977). Formulation and estimation of stochastic frontier production function models. *Journal of Econometrics*, 6, 21–37.

Allais, M. (1943). *A la Recherche d'une Discipline Economique Première Partie, l'Economie Pure*, vol. 1. Paris: Atliers Industria.

Arping, S. (2017). Deposit competition in loan markets. *Journal of Banking and Finance*, 80, 108–118.

Ashenfelter, O.C., Farber, H., and Ransom, M.R. (2010). Labor market monopsony. *Journal of Labor Economics*, 28(2), 203–210.

Bain, J.S. (1956). *Barriers to New Competition*. Cambridge, MA: Harvard University Press.

Battese, G.E., Rao, D.S.P., and O'Donnell, C.J. (2004). A metafrontier production function for estimation of technical efficiencies and technology gaps for firms operating under different technologies. *Journal of Productivity Analysis*, 21, 91–103.

Baumol, W.J., Panzar, J.C., and Willig, R.D. (1982). *Contestable Markets and the Theory of Industry Structure*. San Diego: Harcourt Brace Jovanovich.

Beck, T., Levine, R., and Levkov, A. (2010). Big bad banks? The winners and losers from bank deregulation in the United States. *Journal of Finance*, 65(5), 1637–1667.

Berger, A.N. and Hannan, T.H. (1998). The efficiency cost of market power in the banking industry: A test of the quiet life and related hypotheses. *Review of Economics and Statistics*, 80(3), 454–465.

Berger, A.N., Hasan, I., and Zhou, M. (2009). Bank ownership and efficiency in China: What will happen in the world's largest nation? *Journal of Banking and Finance*, 33, 113–130.

Berger, A.N., Klapper, L.F., and Turk-Ariss, R. (2009). Bank competition and financial stability. *Journal of Financial Services Research*, 35, 99–118.

Bertrand, M. and Mullainathan, S. (2003). Enjoying the quiet life? Corporate governance and managerial preferences. *Journal of Political Economy*, 111, 1043–1075.

Bertrand, M., Schoar, A., and Thesmar, D. (2007). Bank deregulation and industry structure: Evidence from the French banking reforms of 1985. *Journal of Finance*, 72, 597–628.

Bloor, C., Craigie, R., and Munro, A. (2011). The macroeconomic effects of a stable funding requirement. Technical Report, Reserve Bank of New Zealand Paper.

Bogetoft, P., Färe, R., and Obel, B. (2006). Allocative efficiency of technically efficient units. *European Journal of Operational Research*, 168(2), 450–462.

Boyd, J. and De Nicolo, G. (2005). The theory of bank risk taking revisited. *Journal of Finance*, 60, 1329–1343.

Bonin, J.P., Hasan, I., and Wachtel, P. (2005). Bank performance, efficiency and ownership in transition economies. *Journal of Banking and Finance*, 29(1), 31–53.

Brennan, G. and Buchanan, J.M. (1980). *The Power to Tax: Analytical Foundations of a Fiscal Constitution*. Cambridge: Cambridge University Press.

Card, D. and Krueger, A.B. (2015). *Myth and Measurement: The New Economics of the Minimum Wage-Twentieth-Anniversary Edition*. Princeton, NJ: Princeton University Press.

Castiglione, C., Infante, D., and Zieba, M. (2018). Technical inefficiency the Italian performing arts companies. *Small Business Economics*, 51, 609–638.

Chambers, R.G., Färe, R., and Grosskopf, S. (2014). The Lerner Index and economic efficiency. *Theoretical Economics Letters*, 4, 803–805.

Chen, X., Fu, T.-T., Juo, J.-C., and Yu, M.-M. (2020). A comparative analysis of profit inefficiency and productivity convergence between Taiwanese and Chinese banks. *Business Research Quarterly*, 23(3), 193–202.

China Statistical Yearbook (2019). National Bureau of Statistics of China. http://www.stats.gov.cn/tjsj/ndsj/2019/indexeh.htm.

Chow, W.W., Fung, M.K., and Leung, M.-K. (2018). Finance-growth nexus in China from an endogenous switching perspective. *The Journal of International Trade and Economic Development*, 27(4), 443–462.

Chung, Y.H., Färe, R., and Grosskopf, S. (1997). Productivity and undesirable outputs: A directional distance function approach. *Journal of Environmental Management*, 51, 229–240.

Coelli, T., Rao, D.S., O'Donnell, C.J., and Battese, G.E. (2005). *An Introduction to Efficiency and Productivity Analysis*, 2nd edn. New York: Springer.

Degryse, H., Acevedo, A.P.M., and Ongena, S. (2014). Competition in banking. In: Berger, A.N., Molyneux, P., and Wilson, J.O.S. (eds.). *The Oxford Handbook of Banking* (2nd edn.). Oxford: Oxford University Press.

Demsetz, H. (1973). Industry structure, market rivalry, and public policy. *The Journal of Law and Economics*, 16(1), 1–9.

Ding, N., Fung, H.-G., and Jia, J. (2020). Shadow banking, bank ownership, and bank efficiency in China. *Emerging Markets Finance and Trade*, 56, 3785–3804.

Drechsler, I., Savov, A., and Schnabl, P. (2017). The deposits channel of monetary policy. *Quarterly Journal of Economics*, 132, 1819–1876.

Elliott, D.J. and Yan, K. (2013). *The Chinese Financial System: An Introduction and Overview*. Brookings: John L. Thornton China Center.

European Bank for Restructuring and Development (EBRD) (2015). *Transition Report 2015–2016: Rebalancing Finance*. London.

Färe, R. and Grosskopf, S. (1990). A distance function approach to price efficiency. *Journal of Public Economics*, 43, 123–126.

Färe, R. and Grosskopf, S. (1998). Shadow pricing of good and bad commodities. *American Journal of Agricultural Economics*, 80, 584–590.

Färe, R., Grosskopf, S., and Lovell, C.A.K. (1985). *The Measurement of Efficiency of Production*, Ch. 5. Boston: Kluwer-Nijhoff.

Färe, R., Grosskopf, S., and Margaritis, D. (2019). *Pricing Non-marketed Goods Using Distance Functions*, in Collaboration with Robin Sickles, Chenjun Shang, Maryam Hasannasab and William L. Weber. Hanover, MA: NOW Publishers Inc.

Färe, R., Grosskopf, S., and Margaritis, D. (2020). Market Power. mimeo.

Färe, R., Grosskopf, S., and Weber, W.L. (2001). Shadow prices of Missouri public conservation land. *Public Finance Review*, 29(6), 444–460.

Färe, R., Grosskopf, S., and Weber, W.L. (2006). Shadow prices and pollution costs in U.S. agriculture. *Ecological Economics*, 56, 89–103.

Färe, R. and Karagiannis, G. (2017). The denominator rule for share-weighting aggregation. *European Journal of Operational Research*, 260(3), 1175–1180.

Färe, R. and Karagiannis, G. (2021). The Generalized Denominator Rule with Applications. Unpublished Manuscript.

Färe, R. and Primont, D. (1995). *Multi-Output Production and Duality: Theory and Applications*. Boston: Kluwer Academic Publishers.

Färe, R. and Sung, K. J. (1986). On second-order Taylor-series approximation and linear homogeneity. *Aequationes Mathematicae*, 30(1), 180–186.

Färe, R. and Lundberg, A. (2006). Parameterizing the Shortage Function. Unpublished Manuscript, Department of Economics, Oregon State University.

Färe, R., Grosskopf, S., and Tremblay, V. (2012). Market power and technology. *Review of Industrial Organization*, 40, 139–146.

Farrell, M.J. (1957), The measurement of productive efficiency, *Journal of the Royal Statistical Society, Series A, General*, 120(3), 253–281.

Fazioli, R. and Filippini, M. (1997). Cost structure and product mix of local public theatres. *Journal of Cultural Economics*, 21(1), 77–86.

Fernández-Blanco, V., Rodríguez-Álvarez, A., and Wiśniewska, A. (2019). Measuring technical efficiency and marginal cost in the performing arts: The case of municipal theatres in Warsaw. *Journal of Cultural Economics*, 43(1), 97–119.

Fréchet, M.M. (1906). Sur quelques points du calcul fonctionnel. *Rendiconti del Circolo Matematico di Palermo* (1884–1940), 22(1), 1–72.

Frey, B.S. (1997). Has Baumol's cost disease disappeared in the performing arts? *Ricerche Economiche*, 50, 173–182.

Fries, S. and Taci, A. (2005). Cost efficiency of banks in transition: Evidence from 289 banks in 15 post-communist countries. *Journal of Banking and Finance*, 29(1), 55–81.

Fukuyama, H. and Tan, Y. (2019). Deconstructing three-stage overall efficiency into input, output and stability efficiency components with consideration of market power and loan loss provision: An application to Chinese Banks. *International Journal of Financial Economics*. doi:10.1002/ijfe.2185.

Fukuyama, H. and Tan, Y. (2020). A new way to estimate market power in banking. *Journal of the Operational Research Society*. https://doi.10.1080/01605682.2020.1824555.

Fukuyama, H., Devaney, M., and Weber, W.L. (1997). Where East meets West: Frontier estimates of Japanese and U.S. bank productivity. *Fukuoka University Review of Commercial Sciences*, 42(3), 309–331.

Fukuyama, H. and Weber, W.L. (2008). Japanese banking inefficiency and shadow pricing. *Mathematical and Computer Modelling*, 48, 1854–1867.

Fungacova, Z. and Weill, L. (2017). Chapter 8: Bank competition in China. In Bikker, J.A. and Spierdijk, L. (eds.) *Handbook of Competition in Banking and Finance*. Cheltenham and Northampton: Edward Elgar Publishing.

Gao, H., Ru, H., Townsend, R., and Yang, X. (2019). Rise of bank competition: Evidence of banking deregulation in China. NBER Working Paper 25795. National Bureau of Economic Research. www.nber.org/paper/wp/25795.

Gapinski, J.H. (1984). The economics of performing Shakespeare. *American Economic Review*, 74(3), 458–466.

Garcia, D., Kutlu, L., and Sickles, R.C. (2020). Market structures in production economics. In Ray, S.C., Chambers, R.G. and Kumbhakar, S.C. *Handbook of Production Economics*. Singapore: Springer https://doi.org/10.1007/978-10-3450-3 4-1.

Georgescu-Roegen, N. (1951). The aggregate linear production function and its applications to von Neumann's economic model. In *Activity Analysis of Production and Allocation*, pp. 98–115. New York: John Wiley and Sons.

Gurley, J.G. and Shaw, E.S. (1955). Financial aspects of economic development. *American Economic Review*, 44(4), 515–538.

Hausdorff, F. (1914). *Grundzüge der Mengenlehre*, vol. 7. Leipzig: Verlag von Veit.

Havrylchyk, O. and Jurzyk, E. (2011). Inherited or earned? Performance of foreign banks in Central and Eastern Europe. *Journal of Banking and Finance*, 35(5), 1291–1302.

Heider, F., Saidi, F., and Schepens, G. (2019). Life below zero: Bank lending under negative policy rates. *The Review of Financial Studies*, 32(10), 3728–3761.

Hicks, J.R. (1935). Annual survey of economic theory: The theory of monopoly. *Econometrica*, 3, 1–20.

Huang, T.-H., Lin, C.-I., and Chen, K.-C. (2017). Evaluating efficiencies of Chinese commercial banks in the context of stochastic multistage technologies. *Pacific-Basin Finance Journal*, 41, 93–110.

Huang, T.-H., Liu, N.-H., and Kumbhakar, S.C. (2018). Joint estimation of the Lerner Index and cost efficiency using copula methods. *Empirical Economics*, 54, 799–822.

Jia, J. (2016). Efficiency of Chinese banks: A survey and suggested directions for future research. *The Chinese Economy*, 49, 239–256.

Kahn, C., Pennacchi, G., and Sopranzetti, B. (1999). Bank deposit rate clustering: Theory and empirical evidence. *Journal of Finance*, 54(6), 2185–2214.

Karagiannis, G., Midmore, P., and Tzouvelekas, V. (2004). Parametric decomposition of output growth using a stochastic input distance function. *American Journal of Agricultural Economics*, 86(4), 1044–1057.

Keeley, M.C. (1990). Deposit insurance, risk, and market power in banking. *American Economic Review*, 80, 1183–1200.

Klapper, L., Martinez-Peria, M.S., and Zia, B. (2009). Banking in developing nations of Asia: An overview of recent changes in ownership structure. In Berger, A.N., Molyneux, P. and Wilson, J.O.S. *The Oxford Handbook of Banking*. Oxford: Oxford University Press.

Koetter, M., Kolari, J.W., and Spierdijk, L. (2012). Enjoying the quiet life under deregulation? Evidence from adjusted Lerner indices for U.S. banks. *Review of Economics and Statistics*, 94(2), 462–480.

Kopecky, K.J. and Van Hoose, D.D. (2012). Imperfect competition in bank retail markets, deposit and loan rate dynamics, and incomplete pass through. *Journal of Money, Credit and Banking*, 44(6), 1185–1205.

Koutsomanoli-Filippaki, A., Margaritis, D., and Staikouras, C. (2009a). Efficiency and productivity growth in the banking industry of Central and Eastern Europe. *Journal of Banking and Finance*, 33(3), 557–567.

Koutsomanoli-Filippaki, A., Margaritis, D., and Staikouras, C. (2009b). Profit efficiency in the banking industry of Central and Eastern Europe: A directional technology distance function approach. *Managerial Finance*, 35(3), 276–296.

Kumbhakar, S.C. and Lovell, C.A.K. (2003). *Stochastic Frontier Analysis*. Cambridge: Cambridge University Press.

Kutlu, L. and Sickles, R.C. (2012). Estimation of market power in the presence of firm efficiencies. *Journal of Econometrics*, 168, 141–155.

Last, A.-K. and Wetzel, H. (2010). The efficiency of German public theaters: A stochastic frontier analysis approach. *Journal of Cultural Economics*, 34, 89–110.

Last, A.-K. and Wetzel, H. (2011). Baumol's cost disease, efficiency, and productivity in the performing arts: An analysis of German public theaters. *Journal of Cultural Economics*, 35(3), 185–201.

Lerner, A. P. (1934). The concept of monopoly and the measurement of monopoly power. *Review of Economic Studies*, 1(3), 157–175.

Luenberger, D. (1995). *Microeconomic Theory* (International Edition). New York: McGraw-Hill.

Manning, A. (2003). *Monopsony in Motion*. Princeton, NJ: Princeton University Press.

Mantovi, A. (2015). Lerner indexes, productive efficiency and homotheticity. *Economics Letters*, 5(3), 370–374.

Mason, E. (1939). Price and production policies of large-scale enterprise. *American Economic Review*, 29, 61–74.

Musgrave, R.A. and Musgrave, P.B. (1980). *Public Finance in Theory and Practice*, 3rd edn. Singapore: McGraw-Hill.

Neligan, A. (2006). Public funding and repertoire conventionality in the German public theatre sector: An econometric analysis. *Applied Economics*, 38(10), 1111–1121.

Neumark, D. and Sharpe, S.A. (1992). Market structure and the nature of price rigidity: Evidence from the market for consumer deposits. *Quarterly Journal of Economics*, 107(2), 657–680.

OECD. General Government Spending. https://data.oecd.org/gga/general-govern ment-spending.htm.

Panzar, J. and Rosse, J. (1987). Testing for 'monopoly' equilibrium. *Journal of Industrial Economics*, 35, 443–456.

Patrick, H. (1966). Financial development and economic growth in underdeveloped countries. *Economic Development and Cultural Change*, 14, 174–189.

Perloff, J.M., Karp, L.S., and Golan, A. (2007). *Estimating Market Power and Strategies*. Cambridge: Cambridge University Press.

Pindyck, R.S. and Rubinfeld, D.L. (2009). *Microeconomics*, 7th edn. Pearson/Prentice Hall.

Qin, B. and Shaffer, S. (2014). A test of competition in Chinese banking. *Applied Economic Letters*, 21(9), 602–604.

Robinson, J. (1969). *The Economics of Imperfect Competition* (2nd edn.). London: Macmillan.

Rockafellar, R.T. (1970). *Convex Analysis*. Princeton: Princeton University Press.

Rosen, R.J. (2007). Banking market conditions and deposit interest rates. *Journal of Banking and Finance*, 31(12), 3862–3884.

Rosse, J. and Panzar, J. (1977). Chamberlin vs Robinson: An empirical study for monopoly rents. Bell Laboratories Economic Discussion Paper.

Saunders, A., Cornett, M.M., and Erhenjamts, O. (2021). *Financial Institutions Management: A Risk Management Approach*, 10th edn. New York: McGraw Hill.

Schmidt, P. and Lovell, C.A.K. (1979). Estimating technical and allocative inefficiency relative to stochastic production and cost functions. *Journal of Econometrics*, 9, 343–366.

Sealey, C. W. and Lindley, J. T. (1977). Inputs, outputs, and a theory of production and cost at depository financial institutions. *The Journal of Finance*, 32(4), 1251–1266.

Shaffer, S. and Spierdijk, L. (2015). The Panzar-Rosse revenue test and market power in banking. *Journal of Banking and Finance*, 61, 340–347.

Shaffer, S. and Spierdijk, L. (2020). Measuring multi-product banks' market power using the Lerner Index. *Journal of Banking and Finance*, 117. https://doi.org/ 10.1016/j.jbankfin.2020.105859.

Sharpe, S.A. (1997). The effect of consumer switching costs on prices: A theory and its application to the bank deposit market. *Review of Industrial Organization*, 12(1), 79–94.

Shephard, R.W. (1953). *Cost and Production Functions*. Princeton: Princeton University Press.

Shephard, R.W. (1970). *Theory of Cost and Production Functions*. Princeton Studies in Mathematical Economics. Princeton: Princeton University Press.

Solow, R. (1957). Technical change and the aggregate production function. *Review of Economics and Statistics*, 39(3), 312–320.

Spierdijk, L. and Zaouras, M. (2017). The Lerner Index and revenue maximization. *Applied Economics Letters*, 24(15), 1075–1979.

Sun, G. (2020). Banking institutions and banking regulations. In Amstad, M., Sun, G. and Xiong, W. (eds.) *The Handbook of China's Financial System*. Princeton: Princeton University Press.

Taalas, M. (1997). Generalised cost functions for producers of performing arts — Allocative inefficiencies and scale economies in theatres. *Journal of Cultural Economics*, 21(4), 335–353.

Tiebout, C. (1956). A pure theory of local expenditures. *Journal of Political Economy*, 64, 416–424.

Wang, C. and Giouvris, E. (2020). The impact of foreign bank entry on Chinese banks and financial liberalization: Recent evidence. *The Chinese Economy*, 53(2), 177–199.

Weil, D. (2018). Why we should worry about monopsony. Institute for New Economic Thinking, 2.

Wu, C. and Zhang, H. (2019). Competition in the Chinese banking industry: Does Ownership Matter? mimeo.

Yeung, G. (2021). Chinese state-owned commercial banks in reform: Inefficient and yet credible and functional? *Journal in Chinese Governance*, 6(2), 198–231.

Yildirim, H.S. and Philippatos, G.C. (2007). Efficiency of banks: Recent evidence from the transition economies of Europe, 1993–2000. *European Journal of Finance*, 13(2), 123–143.

Zhu, X. (2012). Understanding China's growth: Past, present, and future. *Journal of Economic Perspectives*, 26(4), 103–124.

Zieba, M. (2011). An analysis of technical efficiency and efficiency factors for Austrian and Swiss Non-profit theatres. *Schweizerische Zeitschrift für Volkswirtschaft und Statistik/Swiss Journal of Economics and Statistics*, 147(2), 233–274.

Zieba, M. and Newman, C. (2007). Understanding production in the performing arts: A production function for German public theatres. Resource document: Trinity Economics Papers. Working Paper No. 0707, Trinity College Dublin, Department of Economics. http://www.tcd.ie/Economics/TEP/2007/ TEP0707.pdf. Accessed April 30, 2017.

Zieba, M. and Newman, C. (2013). Organisational structure and managerial efficiency: A quasi-experimental analysis of German public theatres. *Homo Oeconomicus*, 29(4), 497–534.

Index

World Scientific–Now Publishers Series in Business

(Continuation of series card page)

Printed in the United States
by Baker & Taylor Publisher Services